Praise for
Peace: A Case for an Israeli Palestinian Confederation

"The sad history of the Israeli-Palestinian peace process has much to do with the incapacity of the parties to generate innovative ideas, to break away from old patterns. This book, full of creative ideas and original insights, proposes to see the territory Israelis and Palestinians [...] not as divisive but as an opportunity, for they can share i[...] of a confederative system of government. Such [...] the so-far-intractable 'narrative' issues, such [...]
[...] ign minister, Israel

"This is an amazing [...] could not put it down. You can remove the autho[...] substitute any Palestinian with a moderate point of view [...] will and the ideas can represent both."
— *Munther Dajan., dean, Faculty of Arts, Al Quds University, Jerusalem; co-founder, Wasatiyyah (Moderation) movement*

"Joseph Avesar has struggled for years to get his idea for an Israeli-Palestinian confederation to be considered by leaders of both peoples. Now may be the moment, given that the standard two-state concept has withered on the vine. This timely book shows that confederation may not be merely one more option, it may be the best and most humane option for both peoples. Instead of two nation states locked in deadly embrace, why not consider opting for an embrace built on mutual dependency and a common future? Avesar's vision may sound like a fantasy today, but so did Herzl's when he published *Der Judenstat*. This book deserves wide readership, and its ideas deserve serious consideration."
— *M.J. Rosenberg, senior foreign policy fellow, Media Matters*

"... a viable option to an intractable situation, a way out of the peace stalemate in the region. Avesar has presented a strong case, and it deserves a wide public hearing."
— *Mark Juergensmeyer, director of the Orfalea Center for Global & International Studies; professor of sociology and religious studies, University of California, Santa Barbara*

"Sixty two years ago, my friends and I proposed the immediate establishment of a Palestinian state next to the new state of Israel. We believed that the borders between the two states should be open to the free movement of people and goods, and that Jerusalem should be their joint capital. In other words, a kind of confederation. Therefore, Josef Avesar's interesting new book does not shock me. It is well reasoned, logical and sensible. The land between the Mediterranean and the Jordan River is too small to allow for two states with a hermetically sealed border between them. It would condemn both states to a ghetto-like existence. Avesar's new thinking is needed now more than ever."
— *Uri Avnery, peace activist; former member, Irgun and Knesset*

"I continue to believe in a fair two-state solution, with land swaps, that allows both nations a capital in Jerusalem. But Josef Avesar continues to make a careful and thoughtful argument for a democratic Palestinian entity in which confederation plays a central role. His book offers another approach and is welcome in this difficult time when all movement forward is stymied. Even those who do not accept the ultimate logic of his plan will be stimulated and provoked into further thought."
— *Benjamin R. Barber, distinguished senior fellow, DEMOS; Walt Whitman professor emeritus, Rutgers University*

"… a clear and convincing proposal for the upcoming election, via the Internet, of a legislative body representing both Israel and the Palestinian territories. Skeptics may deride it as visionary and unworkable and disagree with some of its specific ideas, but it might later be seen as the first practical proposal to begin the process of achieving that reconciliation and lasting peace for which so many have yearned for so long."
— *Trevor Le Gassick, professor of Arabic literature, University of Michigan*

"Josef Avesar has shown remarkable pragmatism and vision…[His book proposes using] the power of social networking and technology as a means of transcending moribund intergovernmental strategies to build consensus around a novel idea. Avesar is not a vacuous idealist; with remarkable specificity he grapples with all the touchy issues in this intractable conflict."
— *Saleem H. Ali, director, Institute for Environmental Diplomacy and Security, University of Vermont*

"A confederation in Israel and Palestine is the logical solution to the conflict, and *Peace* lays out a practical plan to achieve it. This plan is rooted in equality and justice and provides a way for the people to establish a confederation, with or without their governments. The book is clear and convincing, and anyone interested in achieving peace in the Middle East must read it. This peace plan does not displace others, but is a necessary complement. The confederation solution is not just hypothetical; it includes a path that Israelis and Palestinians and others can take on the voyage toward a resolution."
— *Fred Foldvary, lecturer in economics; director, Civil Society Institute, Santa Clara University, California*

"This book is crucial reading for anyone looking for hope in a conflict that has defied resolution for over a century. Avesar lays out a precise program for doing just the opposite of what the failed Oslo peace process tried to do—bring Israelis and Palestinians together instead of splitting them apart. Whether or not you agree with his arguments, they deserve the widest possible hearing and consideration."
— *Mark LeVine, professor of history, University of California, Irvine; Distinguished Visiting Professor at the Center for Middle Eastern Studies, Lund University, Sweden*

"Inspired with the desire to create conditions for everlasting peace between Israel and Palestine, Josef Avesar, an attorney in the U.S. with a family history that goes back hundreds of years of living with Arabs in Iraq, presents a compelling case for eliminating suspicion, fear and hatred through an inclusive mechanism of confederation."
— *Muhammad Mukhtar Alam, cognitive psychologist; executive director, Centre for Ecological Audit, Social Inclusion and Governance, New Delhi*

"The majority of Palestinians and Israelis truly yearn for peace, but ideology and power have prevented this popular desire from being translated on the ground, leaving occupation, misery and a sense of hopelessness. A confederation is a logical and appropriate solution to the decades-old problem. I praise the persistence of attorney Josef Avesar, who has chosen a winning case to defend, hopefully all the way to peace."
— *Daoud Kuttab, former Ferris Professor of Journalism, Princeton University; director general, PenMedia*

"In a stalled process, to keep pounding on initiatives that failed [will] lead nowhere. Josef Avesar is the new doctor with new medicine. [His] proposal for a confederal outcome to the conflict will resolve the two major issues blocking progress: the future of Jerusalem and virtual borders for Israel and Palestine."
— *Hanna Siniora, publisher,* The Jerusalem Times;
member, Palestine National Council

"Here, finally, is a new approach that would enable both sides, Israelis and Palestinians, to live together yet maintain their separate identities. Over time, and once the advantages and, indeed, the reality of peace and prosperity become clear, it might lead to a unified and egalitarian society. It may be said that the book minimizes the depth of animosity between the two sides, but this has been said for many societies, in the Middle East and elsewhere, where grassroots movements have resulted in remarkable and impressive social progress. The book opens with a wonderful story. It is well worth reading."
— *Nancy Gallagher, professor of history, University of California, Santa Barbara; UC Education Abroad Study Center director for the Middle East*

"In a sea of cynicism, apathy and despair, *Peace* takes a fresh approach. It is time to listen carefully to the ideas presented in this book and concentrate on practical steps. The author bases his concept on decades of experience as a lawyer and is well versed in Arab and Israeli cultures. I hope the book will initiate an intense debate and discussion in Israel, Palestine and the region."
— *Hanoch Guy, emeritus professor, Jewish Studies, Temple University*

"It was a few years ago when Josef Avesar first contacted me; indeed, that was one of my first contacts with Israeli people who believe in peace. For long time I never thought that I could talk to any Israeli because I considered all of them occupiers. For years, the Palestinians followed any hope they thought might solve their problem and bring an end to their suffering; for decades, many proposals have been discussed to solve the Israeli-Palestinian conflict. But until now none of them applied to bring an end to this conflict. One of the realistic solutions and brave ideas is the Confederation. The first time I heard about the idea I received it with big doubt; later I realized that it might be the best idea to be applied to solve this historical issue."
— *Sulaiman Al Hamri, Palestinian; former prisoner of Israel*

"Avesar is a rare individual who understands the motivations that drive Palestinians and Israelis. He advocates for channeling those motivations into peace, prosperity, hope and security for both sides. A must-read book."

— *Mike Ghouse, Muslim activist, frequent guest on Fox News' Hannity show and nationally syndicated radio shows*

"Josef Avesar is not only a dreamer, he is giving us the means to the achievement of his idea."

— *Ouriel Zohar, director, Technion Theatre; visiting professor, HEC and Paris VIII Universties*

"As someone involved in establishing programs designed to foster peace, I became aware of Josef's ideas a few years back when he first proposed an Israel and Palestine confederation. I remember that despite much ridicule, he persisted in developing his concept and getting people to both discuss and support it. This book is a wonderful and very readable presentation of this position. Most importantly, it is a well thought out and constructive contribution to the dialogue on peace."

— *Stephen Sideroff, director, Raoul Wallenberg Institute of Ethics; assistant professor, Department of Psychiatry and Biobehavioral Sciences, University of California, Los Angeles*

"The obvious failure of the two-state solution, from the original U.N. partition plan through Oslo, Madrid, and the current unfolding of an apartheid unitary state, cries out for bold analysis and proposals. Hats off to Josef Avesar for an imaginative initiative to transform the current impasse into a unitary state which retains enough nationalist sympathies on each side to allow confederation to move forward."

— *Dick Platkin, Jews for Peace*

"For more than 60 years, we have lost a significant number of people and spent billions and trillions, yet we have achieved nothing but hostility. The strong logic in [this book] is tremendous."

— *Mohamed Awadalla, Egyptian political activist*

PEACE
A Case for an Israeli Palestinian Confederation

A CASE FOR AN ISRAELI PALESTINIAN CONFEDERATION

JOSEF AVESAR

Damasaja Publishing

PEACE. ©2011 Josef Avesar. All rights reserved.
No part of this book may be used or reproduced in any manner
whatsoever without the written permission of the publisher.

Published by DAMASAJA PUBLISHING
©2011 Josef Avesar

First printing 2011
Printed in U.S.A.

DAMASAJA PUBLISHING
15915 Ventura Blvd., Suite 302
Encino, CA 91436
(818) 783-2934

Author's contact information
josefavesar@sbcglobal.net

Grateful acknowledgment is made to the Washington Institute
of Near East Policy for permission to reprint maps

Book cover design by Michael Kellner
Book design by Elisa Leone
Author's photograph by Ron Finley

ISBN: 978-1-4507-9177-9

Dedication

This book is written in memory of my childhood friend Shmuel Mintus, a brilliant and talented young man with a great sense of humor who lost his life at the age of 19 in the 1973 war.

Contents

Prologue   I
Introduction   V

1   **The Vision of Peace**   1

2   **Israeli Palestinian Confederation**   15
     I.   How could the Israeli Palestinian Confederation resolve difficult questions concerning Jerusalem, the occupation, settlements, refugees and terror?   19
     II.   How could the Confederation succeed in making peace when the Israeli and Palestinian governments cannot?   21
     III.   If there is no trust between the Israeli and Palestinian peoples, how could there be a common government?   22
     IV.   Is it fair for people outside the area to dictate a confederation?   23

3   **What Laws Could the Confederation Pass That the Israeli or Palestinian Governments Were Unable to Pass?**   25
     I.   Ratification of a constitution   27
     II.   Teaching of tolerance and understanding   28
     III.   Joint economic zone   29
     IV.   Common passport   30
     V.   Compensation to Palestinian refugees   31
     VI.   Confederation police force   31
     VII.   Pardon Anwat Breghit   32
     VIII.   Improve relations with Iran   33
     IX.   Redrawing the separation wall   34
     X.   Liaison office between Israel and Palestine   34

XI.	Converting Qalandia checkpoint to an education and commerce center	35
XII.	Emergency legislation to prevent the spread of H1N1 virus in Israel and Palestine	36
XIII.	Construction of a high-speed train connecting Israel and Palestine	37
XIV.	Final-eight soccer competition	38
XV.	Improving construction standards in Palestine and Israel	38
XVI.	Optional civil family laws	39
XVII.	Permanent residency for humanitarian reasons	40
XVIII.	Israeli-Palestinian prisoner exchange	41

4 The Two-State Solution — 43

5 The One-State Solution — 55

6 Could the U.S. Impose Peace? — 63

7 Skeptic's Corner — 89

I.	The Confederation does not have legitimacy	90
II.	The Confederation has no precedent	90
III.	The Confederation is a risk to the Jewish state	91
IV.	The Confederation is not in the long-term interest of the Palestinians	93
V.	The Confederation is a good idea *after* the creation of the two-state solution, not before	94
VI.	Israelis and Palestinians are culturally different	95
VII.	The governments of Israel and Palestine could pass the same legislation, so there is no need for the Confederation	96
VIII.	The governments of Israel and Palestine will ignore the Confederation	98
IX.	Republicans and Democrats do not get along, so how could the Israelis and Palestinians?	99
X.	The Confederation interferes with the sovereignty of Israel and Palestine	100
XI.	Palestinians and Israelis who reside outside the area cannot participate in the elections	102

	XII.	The Confederation was originated by a group outside the area	102
	XIII.	Internet elections are not reliable	103
	XIIII.	Recent developments put the idea of the Confederation into question	104

8   12-12-12   **107**

THE CONSTITUTION OF THE ISRAELI PALESTINIAN CONFEDERATION   **111**

Prologue

In the early 1960s, when my sister Ariela was 16, she and her friend decided to take a swim from the beach in Tel Aviv to one of the ships anchored offshore. In order to understand such an ill-advised decision, one would need to know the state of affairs in Israel at the beginning of the '60s. For the common Israeli, a trip abroad was almost unheard of. People yearned to travel and enjoy the comforts—as we perceived them—that many European and American countries afforded their citizens. Luxury items, automobiles, restaurants and just the everyday feel of modern life fascinated us. In those days Israel was a much simpler place, and the thought of traveling abroad ignited the imagination.

This was the background upon which my sister and her friend decided to "travel abroad" by swimming to the foreign ship that was moored within sight. As teenagers, they did not really plan their "trip." They made the assumption that the ship was close enough for them to reach. They did not contemplate any difficulties they might encounter on reaching the ship, nor whether it would be possible to board it.

With great hopes and aspirations, they started their swim in the salty Mediterranean. Within a few hours my sister's friend gave up and went back. My sister, on the other hand, felt it would be easier to continue all the way to the ship than to swim back to the beach.

My sister never made it to the ship. Her friend was able to swim all the way to shore, and when it started to get dark she became worried and notified the authorities. In the meantime, my sister, alone in the water, was thirsty and hungry and losing her strength. She was lucky to find a floating log to hold onto. She saw the sparkling lights of Tel Aviv in the far distance and knew it would be impossible for her to swim back. As it got darker, my sister rapidly became weaker. She noticed a small, motorized fishing boat within shouting distance and screamed for help, but the men on the boat were not able to hear her due to the sound of its engine.

Luckily, the fishing boat was towing many smaller boats, and a young man seated in the last boat heard her screams. He somehow communicated with the main boat, which circled until the fishermen found my sister holding onto the log and pulled her into the boat. Her entire body was shaking. She collapsed to the floor of the boat as soon as they dragged her from the water. They covered her with towels and blankets, gave her food and water and took her straight to the small port of Tel Aviv, where the police were already waiting.

It turned out that the fisherman were all Israeli Arabs from the city of Acko in northern Israel. Those fisherman knew my sister was Jewish. She was young, attractive, completely at their mercy—and they treated her as one of their own. They saved my sister's life and saved our family from a horrific tragedy that undoubtedly would have remained with my parents and our five other siblings forever.

Several weeks later my sister took me along with her to the city of Acko to thank the owner of the boat and deliver a box of chocolates as a token of her appreciation. Being only 10 years old, I did not appreciate the magnitude of the tragedy that had been averted; I was simply excited to search for the right home with my sister. I recall walking on what appeared to be rooftops from one home to another asking the Arab neighbors for directions to the home of the fisherman who had saved her life. They were all familiar with him, and it was a short search.

It was an emotional moment when we met him and his father, whom I remember vividly. The older man had a round, pleasant face and was warm and friendly to us. We sat on the floor together, and the fisherman's dad spoke softly. All I remember of his message is that it was positive and spiritually uplifting. He probably spoke about cooperation and peaceful coexistence. At that age, I was not fully aware of the problem between Arabs and Jews. I felt a strong emotional connection with the father and with his son, who had saved my sister's life.

After a short visit at the home, the fisherman took my sister and me to a restaurant in Acko. For the first time in my life, I walked in a strange environment among people who were not Jewish and felt completely safe and at peace.

The experience remains embedded in me, and I repeat this story on a regular basis. Often, other Israelis reply with stories of similar experiences. I have learned that stories of Arabs saving Jews and Jews saving Arabs are common, not only in Israel but throughout the entire Arab world.

Introduction

The Internet and today's fast-moving social media accelerate everything. What once took years to accomplish can now take minutes. Information and concepts travel around the globe within seconds. Stereotypical ideas are quickly put down. People travel internationally for business and pleasure on a scale never before seen. Since we now see such a huge variety of people from other cultures, we are learning to judge people based on their personal character instead of what they look like or where they are from. Political and social groups form quickly, many of them transcending religious and national identities.

This globalization of information has become a major factor affecting the Israeli-Palestinian conflict. In the past, when the world was recovering from World War II, events relating to the conflict were not fully discussed in the international arena. Many of the events were considered local news. Meanwhile, both sides were working from two sets of facts, each believing theirs was accurate. The Israelis and the Palestinians were each convinced of their just cause and were oblivious to facts that were significant to the other side.

Today, neither side has a monopoly on facts and ideas because most events in the region are documented and disseminated around the world almost instantaneously. And the world is simply tired of the blame game. At some point the world's public opinion will demand that the Israelis and Palestinians become constructive and put an end to the conflict. One of the possible solutions will be a confederation between Israel and the Palestinians, even if there are no clear lines of demarcation between the two. Eventually, a confederation will become acceptable to both sides, and the major players in the region will have to accept the idea simply because the other resolutions to the conflict, such as the "two-state solution" or the "one-state solution," are much less realistic. Simply stated, a confederation is the least unrealistic solution.

The Israeli Palestinian Confederation proposed in this book is a third government common to Israelis and Palestinians. The Confederation will find acceptance among the Israeli and the Palestinian peoples because it assures that the vital interests of Israel and Palestine are maintained, while at the same time it is flexible and demanding enough to enhance their relationship. The Confederation will be acceptable because it is not meant to replace the current governments but rather to assist them to resolve their differences.

A confederation is the only solution that does not require the destruction of anything. It does not require the dismantling of the states of Israel or Palestine. It does not require the elimination of their armies or other institutions. A confederation only builds upon what already exists. It is based on equality and self-respect. It rejects isolation and embraces dialogue and cooperation. It is not Israeli, nor is it Palestinian; it is both. It is not based on religion or national identify, nor does it reject them. It is based on the necessity of cooperation between two peoples living together in the same land. Palestinians and Israelis can maintain their own national identity, religion, culture and even loyalty to their governments. It is possible to be staunchly "pro-Israel" or "pro-Palestine" and at the same time support the Israeli Palestinian Confederation.

This book is not only about solving old issues between the Palestinians and the Israelis. It is about how the Palestinians and the Israelis can grow and prosper in the future.

I emigrated from Israel to the U.S. immediately after the 1973 war. My parents had immigrated to Palestine from Iraq in the 1930s. They both came from strong Jewish families with roots in Iraq going back hundreds of years. My father was a devout Zionist, which was his motivation to go to Palestine. My mother accompanied him, though she was unmoved by his Zionist ideology.

My father's family was in commerce and the oil business and doing well in Iraq. At the time he left Iraq in 1936 for Palestine, there was not much difference between his family and many of their Arab neighbors. They and their neighbors were mostly secular, sharing the same local

Arabic culture and national identity. Unlike my father, his family saw little future in Palestine. His parents, brothers and sisters, aunts and uncles, remained in Iraq and didn't consider a move to Palestine until after the creation of the state of Israel.

My mother's family was from Baghdad, and like my father's family, they were not Zionists. They were merchants and business people who were not pleased when their daughter moved to Palestine with her husband. Both my parents' families were content in Iraq, and they always described their relationships with the Arab communities as excellent.

I was born in 1953, after the state of Israel was established. I went through the regular educational system in Israel and saw the conflict strictly from Israel's perspective. But as I approached the age of 50, I suddenly went through a huge transformation. I had just returned to my Los Angeles home from a trip to Israel to visit family when I saw a television news report about a suicide bomber who had detonated himself in the same place in Jerusalem where I had sat with my wife and children only a few days before. I saw the umbrellas of the downtown food court where we had eaten. The report was followed by a debate about the bombing. One of the people debating said, "There has to be a solution to this problem. We just can't go on like that. Someone has to come up with a solution." That comment, together with the visual images of the bombing, remained etched in my mind. I realized that the Israeli-Palestinian conflict must be resolved and that neither the Israeli nor the Palestinian governments could bring peace. Several weeks later I woke up with a clear idea that a confederation government mutual to both peoples could pave the road to peace.

The Israeli-Palestinian conflict is a product of miscommunication and lack of understanding by both sides. Both the Israelis and the Palestinians have the same mistrust of each other. They both continue to define their rivalry, and eventually its resolution, in the same one-dimensional formula based on land. Both their governments are unable to come up with a political solution.

Most Jews who now live in Israel are from Arab countries or are descendants of Jews from Arab countries. Many Arabs and Jews have similar features; an outsider who does not know the culture or the language will not be able to point out the differences between them. Most Arabs and Jews in Israel and Palestine are secular. Their food, music and sense of humor are almost identical. Palestinians and Israelis share much of each other's languages; many Palestinians are fluent in Hebrew, and many Jews are fluent in Arabic. They both mix languages regularly. In fact, they use each other's language to express themselves better by borrowing phrases and even adopting each other's curses and blessings.

This is a book about one possible way the Israelis and Palestinians could make peace and grow together into the future. I am not a historian. I am an attorney. In my 30 years of experience I have litigated hundreds of disputes. While each dispute is factually different, the common theme is the same: the emotionally charged litigants are angry, humiliated or jealous.

The facts of the disputes are insignificant compared to the litigants' emotional trauma. I can't remember the number of times that I came back from court after an objective judge or jury had made a decision not to my liking—and yet I'd had to admit that the decision was fair and right. Each time, I regretted my inability to have foreseen and suggested that same solution before we went to court.

When parties enter into a dispute for an emotional reason, those parties are often not able to elevate themselves above the dispute. The natural reaction of a person who is hurt by another is a desire to counter with the same amount of hurt. Most of the energy of the parties is spent fanning the flames of the fire. The greater the emotions, the less rational the parties become and the more their fears magnify. One of the hardest aspects of the lawyer's job is to see things objectively and to convince his or her client to do the same. The Israeli-Palestinian dispute is no different. It has all the emotional elements of a dispute between parties in everyday life. The only difference is the magnitude of the dispute and the fact that it is not going to be decided by a judge or a jury. The dispute will have to be resolved by the Israelis and the Palestinians themselves.

Most of the facts presented here are based on my personal knowledge and what has been provided to me by friends and relatives. The purpose of the book is to show that Israelis and Arabs can live in peace, that the current conflict between them can be overcome. One way is through the creation of a third government mutual to the peoples of Israel and Palestine.

CHAPTER ONE

The Vision of Peace

Peace is the ultimate security for a country. A country cannot rely on its army as the exclusive security measure. A great army can provide a victory and even temporary protection, but not peace. A country at peace does not need an army to defend it. A country at peace would not lose a war because it will not get into a war to begin with. A country at peace need not spend huge amounts of its human and financial resources on its military. When a country is at peace with its neighbors it will not be attacked by them. A country at peace need not spend huge amounts of its human and financial resources on a war. A country at peace has a different state of mind than does a country at war. A country at peace can reach a higher level of existence. It will spend its resources on educating its people, on scientific and medical research and on advancements in the quality of life for its people.

There is something wrong with countries that live for decades in a state of war. There is something wrong when grandparents, parents and children all fight the same war. The war itself becomes their persona. They develop military lingo and phrases. They build a military industry out of proportion to their needs. They constantly search for new wars and new threats. They beget generations of new soldiers and use them like logs feeding a fire. The war and its ancillary industries become an integral part of the country's economy. The war becomes the country's major employer. The war generates "experts" and commentators and demagogues who constantly justify conflict. The war then becomes a self-fulfilling prophecy designed to support its continuation.

The English politician Tony Benn has noted that during war the military becomes the controlling force that shapes public opinion.

"All wars represent a failure in diplomacy," he wrote. The Israeli-Palestinian conflict is proof of that.

One of our Israeli Palestinian Confederation board members, lawyer Nicholas Allis, once said to me that he used to believe that when it comes to peace, our leaders have a plan. He later realized that there is no plan. There are only actions and reactions. This was confirmed to me by Shlomo Ben-Ami, who served as Israel's foreign minister. He told me, "There is no vision for peace; there are no plans for peace."

It took me over 30 years to realize this profound truth. The Israeli and Palestinian governments have shown no vision of peace. They mostly articulate what they do not want to do, or what they want the other government to do, but they rarely state what they are willing to do for peace.

When I discuss the option of an Israeli Palestinian Confederation, I frequently hear the comment, "You know, it takes two to tango." This argument, which is supposed to end the conversation, goes something like this: The Palestinians and the Israelis failed to dance the tango, which proves there cannot be peace between the Palestinians and the Israelis. Only one side wants to tango. The other side will not or is unable to. Therefore, there cannot be peace.

The tango does not have historical or cultural roots in Israel or Palestine. It is not a common dance in that part of the world. In fact, very few people in Palestine or Israel ever dance the tango. It requires specific skills and is (to my taste) a rigid dance. Palestinians and Israelis enjoy much more spontaneous dances in which the whole community can join without any formality or special invitation. The tango should be abolished as a measuring stick for peace between the Palestinians and the Israelis. It limits our vision and constricts our imagination. Why is it necessary to dance the tango as the exclusive method to reach peace? Why can't we dance the debka or the hora? For that matter, why do we need to dance at all? In the same way, do we need to limit ourselves when it comes to peace, one of the most essential aspects of life?

In most human endeavors we do not limit our horizons. We strive to expand our imagination and enlarge our appreciation. We make huge advancements in medicine, science and technology. We learn to approach problems from different, fresh and innovative angles. Governments worldwide write constitutions and treaties to overcome historical animosities, suspicion and hatred. We create monetary systems that transcend individual countries while allowing those countries to maintain their individual identities. However, when it comes to peace between the Palestinians and the Israelis, we limit ourselves to one dimension: the tango. If we can't dance it, no peace.

When I broach the idea of the Israeli Palestinian Confederation, I also get another reaction: "There is no partner for peace." A partnership is one of the most basic and unsophisticated forms of relationship. Partners too often fight and become suspicious of each other and are often unable to grow and prosper because they waste their emotional energy undermining each other.

The legal profession has given us more sophisticated forms of relations because it realizes that sole proprietorships and partnerships are very limited in their scope. No single person and very few partnerships are able to manage huge financial endeavors. We developed the concept of corporation precisely because someone realized that partners cannot raise funds, do research and produce products at a high level all at the same time. The world's stock exchanges have very few, if any, partnerships. I am not suggesting that the Palestinians and Israelis should turn their countries into a corporation. I am only suggesting that the vision of peace should be expanded.

A war or hostility is our failure to solve an issue by being tolerant, creative and smart. A war is usually the least desirable and least successful means of reaching results. When our leaders choose to go to war and we happily support them, we are admitting our failure to innovate.

The normal and truthful question to ask our leaders when we go to war is, "Mr. or Ms. Leader, please explain to us what you did, or failed to do, that now requires us to use the least desirable and least productive method to solve the problem."

If the leaders are honest, their answer should be the following: "We have failed to pay attention to the issue at hand. We have failed to understand how the other side perceived the issue. We have failed to see the issue from their point of view. We have ignored the issue for a long time. We were more concerned about our own issues. We were secretly hoping that the problem would go away. We were hoping that the problem would arise later, when we are not in power. We were blinded by nationalism. We lack imagination."

Of course, none of that will ever happen. Our leaders would not answer in that fashion. But the reality is that this is how many wars break out.

Expanding our vision of peace will remove the personal nastiness, pettiness and animosity. Peace should be the rule. Hostility should be the exception. Hostility is our failure to communicate with each other, to understand the needs of our fellow human beings and to elevate ourselves beyond our immediate concerns. It is our responsibility now, as citizens of the world, to take advantage of the electronic media to connect with each other to forge peace, not only between the Israelis and Palestinians, but also in other parts of the world and perhaps the whole world.

The concept that conflict can be resolved only by governments is a limitation on our vision of peace. The Israeli and Palestinian governments have been at each other's throats for years. They mostly generate their power from a nationalistic base that desires full victory against their enemy. Both governments regularly boast of their success and point out how unreasonable the other government is, but they seldom critically and honestly analyze their own position on peace. Both governments are weak and regularly grasp at straws to survive. Both the Israeli and Palestinian governments treat each other as players in a chess game trying to outsmart the other. They both fail miserably in delivering peace to their people. They both take their people for granted and do not even discuss their vision of peace with them. To think that those governments are the exclusive players who can deliver peace is simply preposterous.

No one person or entity or government can make peace alone. Even if we give governments the benefit of the doubt, they should not be the exclusive players who will make peace. Peace should be a process undertaken by the peoples of both sides. People should be leading the way to peace and should force their own governments to follow. The more people and organizations that participate in the process of creating and maintaining peace, the stronger peace becomes. It should be like a lake with many streams running into it. The more streams that enter the lake, the less likely it is to dry out. Governments could reach a peace agreement, but true peace does not require an agreement. It is a product of substantial cooperation between peoples.

In the context of the Israeli-Palestinian conflict, the new vision of peace requires us to make personal alliances and connections between persons who belong to opposite sides. Just because an Israeli person lives in Tel Aviv and a Palestinian person lives in Gaza, that alone should not make them enemies. The new vision of peace allows both to make interpersonal connections despite their governments' animosity toward each other. The citizens of opposing governments do not necessarily have opposing interests. In fact, they may have similar views and certainly some common interests. Citizens have the responsibility to push their governments to act in their mutual interests, but they can communicate with each other, conduct business and share cultural experiences, even meet with each other in person despite their governments.

In the past, most political constituencies automatically took their government's positions. However, it is now much easier to find people who are willing to put aside their nationalistic feeling and forge peace. They understand that as individuals they must connect with each other, Palestinians with Israelis and Israelis with Palestinians, because isolation from each other perpetuates misunderstanding, prejudice and hatred. They understand that they must connect with each other to keep their own governments in check. They understand that they must connect with each other to keep the dialogue going and to find a common formula for peace.

There are many bereaved parents and families in Palestine and Israel who do not necessarily follow their government's nationalistic point of view. Their attitude is much more global. Because their loved one paid the ultimate price, and because they are living with that calamity, they see the conflict much more realistically. The human tragedy they suffered transcends any nationalistic feeling. Many of them wish to connect with one another regardless of national identity.

There are many Palestinians and Israelis who feel an emotional, cultural or economic connection with each other, even across the borders. Those citizens are the infrastructure and lubricants of peace between their two peoples. They have a new vision of peace that can directly override their own opposing governments.

At one time I interviewed Daniel Pipes, an American conservative thinker. I presented Mr. Pipes with the idea of achieving peace through the Israeli Palestinian Confederation. Mr. Pipes felt that the idea of cooperation between Israelis and Palestinians contradicts history and the matter in which peace is forged. He believes that in order to have peace, either the Israelis or the Palestinians would have to completely win the war over the other, with one remaining as the dominant force.

As will be demonstrated throughout this book, this is a very limited vision of peace. It does not take into account the new communication options available to us for personal connection, including the Internet and electronic devices. We now have much better tools that give us more options than the ones that served military generals, empires and tyrants up to the 21st century.

Would it make sense to limit our health strategies to surgeries and medicine alone? Would it not make sense to also eat right and exercise? There are many people who find natural ways to prevent illnesses and remain healthy. Using this metaphor, the Israeli Palestinian Confederation is the alternative medicine. It is the eat-right-and-exercise aspect of the relationship. It does not proclaim to be the exclusive remedy. Indeed, all remedies and visions should be attempted simultaneously.

There is no one formula to reach peace. Peace is a process that relies on multiple layers of visions and aspirations. It is a process of never-ending and rigorous connections between people on multiple levels. It is a state of mind that needs to be constantly addressed, fed and nurtured.

Does it make sense for either Israelis or Palestinians to believe that they can defeat the other? Does the secret, long-held belief of some that time is on their side really make sense? The January 19, 2009, issue of *Time* magazine contained the population statistics of Jews and Arabs in the state of Israel, the West Bank and Gaza. *Time* noted that there were 5.4 million Jews and 5.5 million Arabs in the entire area in 2008. It estimated that by 2020 the population of Jews would be 6.4 million, and there would be 8.5 million Arabs. Any casual observer will immediately recognize that both peoples are there to stay, and they are not going anywhere anytime soon.

All these millions are firmly embedded in the area, physically, economically and religiously. Both sides have substantial emotional and historical connections to that land. Clearly, neither is going away, and the sooner they learn to live with each other, the better.

The relations between Israelis and Palestinians cannot be described in stark black and white. Many Arabs and Jews have very good relations. It is only when nationalism is thrown into the mix that the relations deteriorate. More importantly, Jews and Arabs inside the state of Israel have had peaceful and growing relations for decades.

For the most part, Arab Israelis and Jewish Israelis live in peaceful coexistence. Arabs participate fully in the Israeli political process. They have their own political parties and Knesset members. Many Arabs participate in the legislative and judicial process. Many are doctors, lawyers, ambassadors or judges. Any person going to an emergency room in any hospital in Israel has an almost equal chance of being treated by an Arab or a Jewish doctor. I heard on Israeli radio that many more Arabs donate body parts to Jews than Jews donate to Arabs or other Jews. On a day-to-day basis, Arabs and Israelis interact with each other peacefully and pleasantly. They buy from and sell to each other and visit each other's homes. They teach each other and learn from each other and attend universities together. Some Arabs even serve in the Israeli army. Many Arabs serve in the Israeli police force and routinely arrest Jews who are suspected of crimes. The reverse is true as well. Arab judges regularly conduct trials where the litigants are Jews, and many Jewish judges conduct trials where Arabs are the litigants. Arabs hire Jewish doctors and lawyers, and the reverse is true as well. All aspects of civic society are mutual to Arabs and Jews within the state of Israel. Arabs are simply an integral part of Israeli society. I am aware of some discrimination that still exists against Arab Israelis, but the relationship between Arab Israelis and Jewish Israelis is far better than the relationship between Israeli Jews and the Palestinians in the West Bank and Gaza.

Nevertheless, Israeli Jews and Arab Palestinians in the West Bank and Gaza are also able to forge meaningful personal relationships. Despite the separation wall and the fences between the two, they are able to communicate by phone, in person and over the Internet. There are many Palestinians in East Jerusalem who are not separated from the Israelis at all. Many of the taxi drivers and hotel workers in Jerusalem are Palestinians who reside in Jerusalem and do not hold Israeli citizenship, yet they work freely in Israel. Many Israelis and Palestinians conduct business with each other on almost all levels. There are hundreds of professional, scientific, peace and trade groups and organizations common to Israelis and Palestinians. The connection between Israelis and Palestinians on a personal and professional level certainly exists. The personal relationships between Jews and Arabs provide the lubricant necessary to keep the peace going. Without that lubricant the prospect of peace is tenuous.

I would argue that the only point of non-agreement is nationalism. In my opinion, most Israelis and Palestinians are secular. Most do not attend synagogues or mosques on a regular basis. Religion, in my opinion, does not divide Israelis and Palestinian as much as nationalism does. In general, both sides feel much greater loyalty and allegiance to their nation than to their religion. The vision of peace should capitalize on human relationships, needs and aspirations rather than focus on the larger disagreements of nationalism.

An Israeli Palestinian Confederation will help provide both sides with one more common ground: a shared identity. They will share a common government: the government of the Israeli Palestinian Confederation. It is possible for an Israeli or a Palestinian to be proud of and nationalistic toward his own government and at the same time be proud of and loyal to a shared or common government such as the Israeli Palestinian Confederation.

A vision of peace could include the expansion of the individual vision of each Palestinian and Israeli as a common expression through a unified government that does not contradict their separate governments. They currently have no mutual, common framework to express this relation. Many Israelis and Palestinians have a higher loyalty and sense of friendship to each other than to neighbors with whom they share the same citizenship. The Israeli Palestinian Confederation will help them capitalize on their trusting relationships and help propel other segments of society that are perhaps more reserved and suspicious to support the common government. Those Arabs and Jews who trust each other today will be the pioneer members of the Israeli Palestinian Confederation.

What could peace between the Israelis and the Palestinians look like? In order to have peace it will be necessary to reduce the level of nationalism. This would mean that an Israeli or a Palestinian could feel a strong connection to his or her country but would not define the love for country in terms of animosity to the other side.

A vision of peace takes into consideration the special needs of the Israeli and Palestinian peoples. It encourages and rewards cooperation while preventing one side from taking advantage of the other. It encourages generosity between its participants while discouraging pettiness and triviality. It encourages transparency and open dialogue while rejecting secrecy.

This vision of peace for the Israelis and Palestinians assumes trust and cooperation. Palestinians and Israelis will eventually feel safe with each other and respect each other's religious and holy sites. They will maintain their separate national identity and language but will be able to share culture and commerce. They will deal with the painful past and fully accept and admit their mistakes. They will create a system where most of their common issues will be dealt with in a transparent and democratic manner. The Israelis and the Palestinians will eventually reach the point where they recognize that a system of cooperation enables a far better quality of life for both. They will recognize not only their common cultural background but also their mutual strategic interest.

A realistic peace could be defined in terms of multiple layers of jurisdiction. This is common in many countries in the world, including the U.S. and Europe. Having multi-layer jurisdictions is a practical way to preserve the special feelings and attachments people have toward an idea or territory, including religious identity, while reciprocating the same respect to those who do not share the same sentiments. It is a mechanism to overcome differences and suspicion between peoples of different backgrounds or national ideology while allowing them to maintain their own unique identities.

Many of us live and function very well within a system of multi-layer jurisdictions. Our home is the first jurisdiction. We each have our own rules and customs in our homes. When someone else enters our home, she or he must obey our rules and honor our customs. We then look to our homeowners association. The rules of our homeowners association apply only to those who belong to the association or enter the association territory. We then look to our city. Each city has its own ordinances and laws, which may differ from other cities. When we reside in or visit a city, we must abide by that city's rules. Each state has its own laws. The residents or visitors to the state must comply with that state's laws. The residents of a nation must comply with that government's overarching laws.

A constitution provides the framework for separate governments to work independently of each other. It provides certain guidelines that allow those governments to maintain their identities and individual aspirations but at the same time preserve the overall needs of the entire nation. A constitution also creates a mechanism to resolve conflicting laws and determines how those laws will be interpreted. A constitution provides for such basic values as freedom of speech and right of assembly, which must be protected at all times for all people. A constitution provides for the individual's equality and protection under the law. I have always believed that America's success is based on the legal system that is founded in the U.S. Constitution.

Most Jews who arrived in Palestine, and subsequently Israel, came from autocratic countries in Europe and the Middle East. Most had never experienced democracy or democratic elections. Likewise, Palestinians never experienced a democracy and never voted in an election until very late in the 20th century. Israeli Arabs did not participate in democracy until the creation of the state of Israel.

The process of adaptation when people move from autocratic countries to democracies is well documented. They seem to accept the democratic values right away, and with enthusiasm. Most Israelis and Palestinians are secular and open to democratic principles. The creation of a common government for both peoples together, as long as it does not conflict with their own national government, is likely to be adopted by both.

The recent strong democratic expression in Egypt, Tunisia, Yemen, Syria, Libya, Palestine and Israel could have a positive effect on the formation of an Israeli Palestinian Confederation. People of the Middle East are demanding democracy for themselves rather than abandoning their own country and moving to democratic countries. They are taking on a great task: to convert thousands of years of autocracy into a new form of government. The recent demonstrations now known as the Arab Spring were started by a few young people who connected with each other through social media and who were able to influence thousands. This shows not only technological sophistication but also intellectual vision. These movements are a classic example of the 2 percent solution, in which a small minority motivates or affects a much larger population.

Like most people, I was mesmerized by the upheavals and particularly by the genuine expression of democratic values. I remember watching an interview with a young demonstrator who said the goal of their movement is to create a democratic government that emphasizes institutions over individuals, and that the people are tired of being dependent on individuals interested only in their political control and not the well-being of the people.

It is clear that a large segment of the Middle East, including Israel and Palestine, has an educated, secular population that has already accepted democracy. Many of them travel regularly around the world and read foreign literature and newspapers. Their level of sophistication in technology, science and governance is rising by the minute. The people of the Middle East, including the Israelis and Palestinians, are eager to push their governments to a higher level of democracy.

Governments should protect the right of their people to exercise their religion and to enjoy the spiritual fulfillment it provides. The holy sites sacred to all religions should be protected vigorously and free access to them must be uninterrupted. However, the convergence of religion and nationalism tends to perpetuate extremism and alienate people on both sides. Nationalism should not rely on religion as a source of support. Nationalism should be defined as a source of pride and a symbol of achievement and excellence, not in terms of religious differences. Religion should be a source of solace and personal satisfaction, not a reason to inflame hatred.

Israel is strong and militarily secure enough to take on a new challenge. This challenge is to make peace with the Palestinians and with Arabs, just as it made peace with Europe, where Jews suffered the worst anti-Semitism and the Holocaust.

If Israel wants to maintain itself as a Jewish state, it has a much greater chance of doing so when it is at peace with the Palestinians and its Arab neighbors. It cannot forever remain in a state of war and maintain its Jewish identity.

Many who object to the idea of a confederation do so thinking that Israel can remain a Jewish state only if it remains in a state of war with the Palestinians and its Arab neighbors. They claim that a state of peace with the Arabs will cause assimilation of Jews and Arabs and will destroy the nation's Jewish character.

Could Israel remain a Jewish state if it makes peace with the Palestinians? I believe the answer is yes. However, Israel must be willing to accept new formulas that recognize the need to cooperate with the Palestinians without risking its own vital interests. It must be willing to expand its views beyond the formula of the "two-state solution." The Palestinians must also expand their views and adopt other formulas for peace. As shown in this book, the "two-state" and "one-state" solutions have not been successful up to now for various reasons. A confederation government is not inconsistent with any formula those governments pursue. A confederation is an adjunct to those formulas.

For thousands of years Jews survived the Diaspora, even under the constant threat of anti-Semitism. I believe Jews will flourish even more in Israel when peace comes about. However, Israel must come up with an acceptable constitutional and legal framework to validate a Jewish state within the international community. It must protect its Arab minorities and prepare for the inevitable day that the Arabs become the majority. It must create an atmosphere of fair and positive economic competition with its own Arab citizens and neighbors as well as those abroad. Israel must plan on maintaining its status as a Jewish state, not because it controls the laws and the guns, but because the Jews living there will be excellent contributors to its society. It must deal honestly with the Palestinian issue and the Palestinian refugees. It also must come up with a solution to the challenging relationship between secular and religious Jews.

Israel has scores of individuals with the intellectual capabilities and rationality to take on these challenges. However, I have my doubts when it comes to politicians who thrive on delivering one more military victory for the Jewish state. No current leaders are willing to take risks for peace if it requires shedding their military egos.

A country must learn to stand on its own. It must have substantive depth to its existence. It cannot define itself in terms of its enemies. I believe that Israel has that substance. It is the place where the world's three major religions—Judaism, Islam and Christianity—are part of its very fabric. It has a rich history going back thousands of years, which is on display in almost every city. It is the home to the ancient Hebrew and Arabic languages that are used today as they were thousands of years ago. It has its unique culture of literature, music and food. It is a tremendous contributor to science, industry, agriculture and the prosperity of the world.

The Palestinians are facing the same challenges. They mostly define themselves in relation to Israel. They have the same fear of peace. They also believe that peace will open the path to assimilation and intermarriage with Jews. Many Palestinians also feel safer when the two peoples are isolated from each other. Palestinians also have their own rich culture, religion and language going back thousands of years.

I often ask my Arab and Jewish friends the same question: Do you want your son or daughter to marry someone of the other religion? Almost always, both my Jewish friends and my Arab friends respond in the negative. I then ask the next question: Are you willing to have your son killed so that your daughter will not marry outside the faith?

In the context of peace, this is a choice every Israeli or Palestinian will eventually have to make. Is it more important to separate the two peoples so they do not assimilate, or is it more important to have peace with the chance of intermarriage and assimilation between faiths as part of the deal?

A nation does not and should not be in the business of making these kinds of choices for its people. These are individual issues for every family to address privately. Jews and Muslims in the U.S. and other countries face these issues without engaging in a war of religion with each other. A country should not be in the matchmaking business, and it should not perpetuate war to isolate its people from others. When these issues finally surface in a blunt and vivid manner, most Israelis and Palestinians will choose peace over religious isolation.

The Israeli Palestinian Confederation is an excellent tool to help the Palestinians and the Israelis reach peace and create a constitutional framework to maintain Israeli and Palestinian identities and core values. Along with a large segment of both societies, I believe the Israelis and the Palestinians have enough in common to build a foundation of trust.

Those commonalities include mutual secularism and mutual religious orthodoxy. They also include a common culture and desire for peace. The Israeli Palestinian Confederation offers a platform for those commonalities to propel the cause of peace.

CHAPTER TWO

Israeli Palestinian Confederation

The Israeli Palestinian Confederation is simply an independent government mutual to the Palestinian and Israeli peoples. To understand the concept better, it may be worthwhile to understand what the Confederation is not. It is not the exclusive government in the region, and it is not a super-government above the governments of Israel or Palestine. It does not replace the separate Israeli or Palestinian governments. It does not require the abolishment of Israeli or Palestinian institutions, such as the army or police. It does not require the Palestinian or Israeli governments to change their political agendas or national identity. It does not require the Palestinian or Israeli governments to stop their negotiations with each other.

The Confederation is an additional government representing the Palestinian and the Israeli people together. It is a supplemental government. It will be elected by the Palestinians and the Israelis together, and it will be based on a system of three branches of government. The Confederation Parliament will pass laws, but those laws will be subject to a veto by the separate Palestinian and Israeli governments.

Under the Confederation Constitution, there will be 300 members of Parliament representing 300 districts in Israel, the West Bank and Gaza. In order for the 300 representatives to pass a piece of legislation, 55 percent of the Israeli and 55 percent of the Palestinian members of Parliament must vote "yes" on that legislation.

Both the legislative and executive branches of the Israeli and Palestinian governments will have veto power over the Confederation's legislation. If those governments veto the legislation, it will not become law. However, if they decline to veto, the legislation will become law.

According to the Constitution, elections to Parliament shall take place within the state of Israel, the West Bank and Gaza. To be eligible to vote, a person must be a citizen and a resident of Palestine or Israel and have attained the age of 18 years. The voter must reside in Israel or Palestine at the time of the election and must be physically within Israel or Palestine when he or she votes.

To be elected to Parliament, a person must be at least 21 years of age and a resident and citizen of Israel or Palestine and must have resided for at least 180 days in the district in which he or she made the bid for candidacy.

The president and vice president must be citizens of Israel or Palestine and must be at least 35 years of age. The president serves for two years and then rotates that office with the vice president. If the president is a Palestinian citizen, the vice president must be an Israeli citizen. The person who receives the most votes will be the first to serve as president. The person of the opposite citizenship who receives the next largest number of votes becomes the vice president. Both the president and the vice president must reside in Israel or Palestine prior to the elections.

The number of Palestinians or Israelis elected to Parliament is less important than the ratio needed to pass legislation: 55 percent of the Palestinian and 55 percent of the Israeli members will have to vote "yes." Even if the Israelis have more representatives, they will not be able to pass legislation without the consent of at least 55 percent of the Palestinian representatives. The number of Palestinian and Israeli representatives may change in the future depending on population growth.

Initially, the Parliament and the entire Confederation will discuss and meet predominately over the Internet, which will help overcome any travel restrictions. In addition, the discussions and voting will be completely transparent. The whole world will be able to see the postings and how each Parliament member voted.

Election to Parliament is based on districts. A voter will be able to cast a ballot for any candidate in his or her district regardless of the nationality of the candidate. Some districts will be entirely Palestinian or Israeli, and some will be mixed. In mixed areas, such as Jerusalem, an Israeli may vote for a Palestinian candidate, and a Palestinian may vote for an Israeli. Both Israelis and Palestinians will be able to vote for candidates for the presidency and vice-presidency regardless of nationalities.

The Confederation will also have a judicial branch. Article III, Section 1 of the Constitution says: "The judicial power of the Israeli Palestinian Confederation shall be vested in one Supreme Court and in such lower courts as the Parliament may from time to time ordain and establish. There shall be an equal number of Israeli and Palestinian Judges. Each trial shall contain the same number of Israeli and Palestinian Judges. All Judges for the Israeli Palestinian Confederation shall be appointed equally by the President and Vice President and shall be confirmed by the Parliament." This is meant to assure both sides that there will be fairness at trial and that Israelis and Palestinians will have equal number of judges appointed and serving at each trial.

In addition, the Constitution grants the power of the judges to deal only with statutes passed by the Confederation or to interpret the Constitution itself. This means that they cannot rule on any internal issues or laws of the Israeli or Palestinian governments.

Article III, Section 3 protects the citizens of each government from the possibility that the judges of the other nationality will decide against him or her for a nationalistic reason. It says, "… any legal decision against a Palestinian or Israeli citizen or entity must have a majority of Judges of the same citizenship as that of the person or entity against whom a decision is rendered." This means that in order for a Palestinian or an Israeli to have an adverse decision, there must be a majority of judges of their nationality who will decide against them.

The Constitution provides yet another safeguard to both Israeli and Palestinian citizens. Article III, Section 4 provides that "All legal decisions, except those relating to the internal operation of the Confederation government, shall have an automatic 60-day stay, and may be appealed to the separate Israeli or Palestinian judicial systems, and may be subject to a complete or partial reversal or modification by the respective Palestinian or Israeli courts in accordance with their laws and requirements." This means that an Israeli or Palestinian who feels that the majority judges (of his or her nationality) wrongly decided the case has 60 days to appeal to the separate court system of that individual's government to overturn the adverse decision against him.

IPC LEGISLATIVE PROCESS

Israeli Government Veto Power

Palestinian Government Veto Power

- Executive Branch
- Legislative Branch
- Executive Branch
- Legislative Branch

STEP ONE ↓

Bill is introduced
IN THE 300-MEMBER CONFEDERATION PARLIAMENT

STEP TWO ↓

To pass, the bill must receive YES votes from
55% OF ISRAELI MEMBERS AND
55% OF PALESTINIAN MEMBERS

STEP THREE ↓

If bill passes
IT IS SUBMITTED TO THE GOVERNMENTS OF ISRAEL AND PALESTINE

STEP FOUR ↓

Legislative waiting period
TO SEE IF THE ISRAELI OR PALESTINIAN EXECUTIVE OR LEGISLATIVE BRANCHES [SEE ABOVE] ISSUE A VETO

STEP FIVE ↓

If no veto
BILL BECOMES LAW

18 PEACE

I
How could the Israeli Palestinian Confederation resolve difficult questions concerning Jerusalem, the occupation, settlements, refugees and terror?

The Confederation is an independent government. It is not entirely Israeli, nor is it entirely Palestinian. It will be a government for both people together, made up mutually by Israelis and Palestinians. This will mean that it is answerable to both peoples, not just one. One of the reasons for its creation is that it will be able to suggest options that are mutually beneficial. It will be able to suggest compromises that neither the Israeli nor the Palestinian governments could suggest on their own. In fact, one of the main functions of the Confederation will be to come up with resolutions that are not politically tenable to the separate governments of Israel or Palestine, but that those governments would consider realistic if implemented by a third government.

The Confederation will have the flexibility to create a mutual police force comprised of equal numbers of Israelis and Palestinians. This police force will have its own distinct uniform and be managed by an equal number of Israeli and Palestinian officers. It will have a set of procedures ensuring that it will not override Israeli or Palestinian sovereignty, and it will be assigned to protect people and jurisdictions specifically designated in legislation acceptable to the Israeli and Palestinian governments. It will have checks and balances from both perspectives because it will be manned by both Israeli and Palestinian citizens. This police force is less likely to be hostile to the Israelis or the Palestinians because it will be comprised of Israeli and Palestinian police officers speaking Hebrew and Arabic. The police will be able to communicate with the people of both sides and will be familiar with their culture and mannerisms and sensitive to their special needs. The police will not be viewed as occupiers but rather as law enforcement for the community. It will be a regular police department serving a community that happens to be a mixture of Palestinians and Israelis.

This police force could have huge significance in helping to solve the issues of the occupation, Jerusalem and terror. The Confederation police, with the agreement of the governments of Israel and Palestine, will be able to assert jurisdiction in specific areas, such as common religious sites in Jerusalem.

They will be able to man certain checkpoints and joint economic zones. They will be able to work hand in hand with the Israeli and Palestinian military and police forces.

Palestinians currently view the Israeli army and border police as an occupying force. They strongly resent the presence of this force and question its legitimacy and necessity. They view the Israeli military as an adversarial force mostly designed to harass them. The relationship between Palestinian civilians and the Israeli army and border police is one of suspicion and resentment.

A Confederation police force made of equal number of Israelis and Palestinians will not be viewed by either side with the same amount of resentment and suspicion. A professional Confederation police force will treat both peoples equally and fairly and be much less likely to provoke animosity and draw attacks.

The Confederation will also be able to make suggestions and propose legislation that neither the Israeli or Palestinian governments dare bring up on their own. For example, on the question of the Palestinian refugees and the right of return, the Confederation Parliament may suggest a reasonable compensation to the refugees and a right of return to a limited number of refugees. Neither the Israeli nor the Palestinian government, for internal political reasons, will have the guts to make such a suggestion. However, if the Confederation brings it up and it turns out that both the Israeli and Palestinian populations are receptive to this solution, the separate governments of Israel and Palestine will "reluctantly" go along.

The Confederation could also pass legislation regarding the settlements that will be acceptable to the separate governments of Israel and Palestine. It may want to deal with each settlement separately. It may agree that some settlements need to be removed and some should stay. It may agree on greater cooperation between the settlements and the Palestinian population in the form of joint economic zones that could improve and expand relationships and reduce tension. It may provide for incentives and financial compensation for the settlers to move out and sell their homes to Palestinians in exchange for expanding other settlements. It may provide for legislation regarding common infrastructure systems between the settlers and the Palestinians to expand and improve their roads, utilities and sewer systems. It may also utilize the Confederation police force to help manage and improve the relationship between the settlers and Palestinians.

It is hoped that the Confederation government will make any conflict a boring one. It will deal with issues in an intricate and detailed matter. It will meet daily over the Internet to discuss issues such as traffic, sewer systems, pipes, drainage systems, hospitals and schools, bridges, fences, water rights, etc. It will present scientific reports and environmental studies. It will discuss the most mundane issues, similar to what local governments do every day all over the world. In all likelihood, those issues will be so tedious that no terrorist would want to derail them.

The reader should be reminded that the Confederation does not preclude separate agreements between the Israeli and Palestinian governments. Those governments will be encouraged to find their own peaceful solutions.

II

How could the Confederation succeed in making peace when the Israeli and Palestinian governments cannot?

Traditionally, the Israeli and Palestinian governments have dealt with each other as adversaries. They represent the national interest of their people and therefore have conflict. As an independent government mutual to Palestinians and Israelis, the Israeli Palestinian Confederation must solve issues in a way that will be acceptable to both sides. Both governments dedicate a fraction of their time dealing with the issue of peace. The Confederation's entire purpose is to make peace.

Traditionally, both the Israeli and Palestinian governments have had dual and often conflicting tasks. Many times those governments have had to appease constituents who demanded that their government be tough toward the other side, making flexibility difficult. However, the Confederation's constituents are Palestinians and Israelis who demand one thing only: peace. The Confederation does not have dual or conflicting tasks.

Many times, negotiations between the Israeli and Palestinian governments are in and of themselves a catalyst for violence. Violence is used frequently as a means to derail their negotiations or agreements. However, the Confederation's legislative work will take place between the 300 Parliament members over the Internet on a daily basis.

The issues and voting will mostly be mundane and incremental. In all likelihood, Parliament members will not deal with volatile issues in one vote and therefore will not attract efforts to derail their work. The Confederation will have certain tools that have never been available to either the Israeli or Palestinian governments:

Objectivity *The Confederation is an independent government for both the Palestinians and Israelis; it is designed to solve issues in a manner that is beneficial to both peoples.*

Sustainability *The Confederation is exclusively designed to negotiate agreement among its Parliament members; it has no purpose other than to discuss these issues daily and resolve them by peaceful means.*

Flexibility *Because the Confederation is an independent government for both Palestinians and Israelis, it has greater flexibility to suggest innovative or partial solutions that have not been suggested by the separate Palestinian or Israeli governments.*

Accessibility *Because the Confederation is comprised of Palestinians and Israelis together, it will have greater access to governments and individuals, access that is now being denied to one side or the other, or to both.*

The Confederation is a facilitator designed to find common ground between the Palestinian and Israeli governments. It is an extra tool to improve peoples' lives that is not otherwise available. The Confederation will constantly explore methods to achieve peace and force the separate Israeli and Palestinian governments to deal with issues in ways they were heretofore unable or unwilling to attempt because of their own national or political structure.

III

If there is no trust between the Israeli and Palestinian peoples, how could there be a common government?

The Confederation government is created in such a way that cooperation by both sides is essential. It has multiple layers of checks and balances so that one side does not dominate the other. This system of governance requires cooperation. Without cooperation, nothing gets done. For example, in order for its Parliament to pass legislation, at least 55 percent of the Palestinian members and at least 55 percent of the Israeli members must vote "yes." If either side disagrees, the legislation cannot pass. Subsequent to the legislation's passage, the Constitution grants the Israeli and Palestinian heads of state and legislatures an opportunity to veto the legislation.

Should any one of them veto the legislation, it cannot pass. There are many other examples of checks and balances spelled out in the Confederation Constitution. Those checks and balances will compel both sides to engage with each other constantly and at the same time negotiate with the two separate governments to address their concerns. This process of constant negotiation will eventually give birth to narrow legislation that "squeezes" from both sides the one thing they both agree upon. Months or years down the line, they may recognize that they can broaden the legislation and may agree to expand it. The constant discussions will have a positive snowball effect on the dialogue between Israelis and Palestinians. It will be the first time in history that Israelis and Palestinians, representing their particular districts, will meet together as equals and discuss intricate solutions to benefit the needs of all.

IV

Is it fair for people outside the area to dictate a confederation?

Individuals, governments, and other entities worldwide have attempted to influence events in this region. In fact, the idea for the state of Israel was conceived outside the region. The Israeli-Palestinian conflict has grown to global proportions, with people all over the world affected by the hostilities. This conflict is discussed and written about daily in media worldwide. Israelis and Palestinians are scattered all over the planet, yet they maintain strong emotional, political and economic ties to the region. Organizations and private parties worldwide are constantly lobbying their governments in an effort to influence decisions in the area.

The Israeli and Palestinian governments have failed for decades to reach a resolution and in many cases have made the situation worse. The Israeli and Palestinian peoples are engulfed in the conflict, and many times it is hard for them to see things objectively. Sometimes a fair and reasonable approach to a conflict is seen more clearly from the outside.

CHAPTER THREE

WHAT LAWS COULD THE CONFEDERATION PASS THAT THE ISRAELI OR PALESTINIAN GOVERNMENTS WERE UNABLE TO PASS?

It is important to understand that the Israeli Palestinian Confederation is a separate entity from the Israeli and Palestinian governments and thus has a unique outlook. Those governments pass laws that, in their view, are good for their own people, but they mostly do so without regard for the other. The Confederation will not be able to pass legislation unless it benefits both sides. Any legislation that is contrary to the needs of both peoples either will not pass the Parliament or will certainly be vetoed by the Palestinian or Israeli heads of state or legislatures. The Confederation must therefore maneuver a very rocky terrain before it can effect any legislation. Despite those hurdles, there are areas of human endeavor that can be legislated for the benefit of both peoples without meeting a swift veto by the Israeli or Palestinian governments.

To see how the Confederation might negotiate some of the region's most contentious issues, we conducted an experiment on Facebook that lasted almost two years. We created a mock Confederation government. We also had a mock president of Palestine, a mock Israeli prime minister and a mock Hamas leader. We had volunteers, both Israeli and Palestinian, who agreed to act as the Confederation's Parliament members. The aim was to see if it would be possible to reach consensus between Israelis and Palestinians. We also wanted to know if it would be possible to reach a middle ground that neither the Israeli nor the Palestinian leaders would veto.

The main advantage of the process was that all discussion was public. An open and transparent discussion required participants to think twice before they aired their point of view. It is much easier to be a bigot or remain close-minded when one preaches to the choir. However, it is quite different when a person voices opinions in public to those who are not necessarily from the same camp.

At the beginning of the mock Confederation, there was tremendous amount of blaming and "shouting" between the pro-Israeli and pro-Palestinian sides. However, once they understood that they were really on the same side and that the purpose of the Confederation government was to enhance the lives of both Israelis and Palestinians, it became much easier to pass legislation. The mock Parliament members underwent a dramatic transformation when they understood the advantages given them by the new rules of the game. In the beginning, it was difficult for them to understand that they didn't represent the entire country of Israel or Palestine and that they weren't necessarily each other's enemies. Their task was to understand that they would have to compromise with each other and become practical. Many, probably the majority, ultimately understood the concept of meeting the other side halfway for the benefit of both.

The mock president had a large role to play. He continually had to remind the Parliament members that they represented one district and not the entire nation of Israel or Palestine, and that the interests of the Israeli and Palestinian governments were already represented by separate Israeli and Palestinian leaders. He also had to negotiate with those leaders and pressure them to accept reasonable legislation, and on many occasions he was successful.

I recall that one of the issues that arose immediately was whether to allow the Hamas leader a veto power over legislation relating to Gaza. Many Parliament members, both Israelis and Palestinians, thought that was a bad idea. However, the majority finally voted to allow the Hamas leader that veto. The thought behind the majority vote was that if the Hamas leader were ignored, the entire Gaza Strip would be ignored. It was more sensible to include the Hamas leader in the discussion and give him a veto power so that he would be responsible for and participate in legislation relating to the Gaza Strip. At the end of the day, as I recall, the mock Hamas leader did not veto a single measure and accepted all the legislation passed by the Confederation.

At one point, the mock Palestinian president wanted to veto the Confederation Constitution. However, his attempt was rejected by the Parliament, which had to explain politely that he had no standing to veto the Constitution as the Confederation is a separate entity from his government. He finally backed off, realizing that he was stepping beyond his jurisdiction.

When the real Confederation government is created, much of what played out in the experiment will be repeated. In the real world, the separate Palestinian and Israeli governments will quickly recognize that legislation passed by the Confederation Parliament to enhance and improve the relationship between the two peoples should not be vetoed. Such a veto will be against the interest of their people. The whole world will condemn a veto if it negates the interest of peace. A veto by an Israeli or Palestinian government contrary to the cause of peace will expose that government as a warmonger acting against the interest of its own people. A government that would veto such legislation would suffer world condemnation, with all the obvious political and economic implications. Here's how the Facebook experiment worked out:

I
Ratification of a constitution

The Confederation's mock Parliament was able to adopt a constitution that recognized the government of Israel as the legitimate government of the Israeli people and the government of Palestine as the legitimate government of the Palestinian people. The mock legislators accepted the notion that the Confederation's purpose is to resolve conflicts and to expand the relationship between Palestinians and Israelis. The Parliament accepted the idea of equality between the Israelis and Palestinians and the idea that both are entitled to equal rights under the law and are guaranteed human rights and freedom.

The foundation of the Constitution is that the creation of the Confederation is consistent with the aspirations of the peoples of Palestine and Israel and does not intend to supersede or supplant their respective governments. The mock legislators accepted the mechanism of a 300-member Parliament, each member representing a district, and the requirement that 55 percent of its Israeli members and 55 percent of its Palestinian members would need to vote "yes" before any legislation could pass. They accepted the idea that both the Israeli and Palestinian heads of government and those nations' legislatures would have veto power over this legislation.

The mock legislators agreed in principle on a common formula that was acceptable to both the Israelis and Palestinians. They agreed to create a government that would serve "below" the governments of Israel and Palestine, and that it would be a government dedicated to peace. They accepted the idea of separation of powers between the legislative, executive and judicial branches. They accepted that the Confederation's government would be secular rather than religious, based neither on Judaism nor Islam, nor any other religion.

Many Palestinians and Israelis who live in Israel, the West Bank and Gaza are willing to accept these same constitutional foundations and principles. They realize that this Constitution is an acceptable formula that helps the sides move forward without the need to abandon their loyalty to their principles. In fact, in order to take office in the Confederation, one would have to swear allegiance to the Confederation Constitution. This document seems to be acceptable to both Israelis and Palestinians without any meaningful objections. The neutrality of the Constitution and the fact that it treats both sides as equals will make it acceptable to reasonable people. The Constitution is found at the end of this book for the reader's review.

II
Teaching of tolerance and understanding

The Confederation's mock Parliament passed legislation to require both Palestinian and Israeli educational systems to teach tolerance in their public schools. The legislation required that both educational systems devote a certain number of hours for both sides to teach the history of the other. The Israeli public education system was required to teach Palestinian history and the Palestinian public education system to teach Israeli history. Both systems were required to work on a specific mutual curriculum. Israeli and Palestinian educators would draft textbooks together and arrange for a regular exchange of teachers. There was a requirement that Palestinian teachers would visit Israeli schools to present the Palestinian view of history and that Israeli teachers would do the equivalent. Public television on both sides was required to carry a certain number of hours per week of balanced broadcasting to teach those subjects. The Confederation would be the facilitator that would ensure that both sides' educational material was fairly presented and acceptable.

Lack of knowledge of each other's history creates a bottomless pit of hostility, inhibiting any possibility of mutual understanding or future cooperation. Lack of knowledge contributes to isolation and suspicion of one another. It perpetuates primitive hatred, which penetrates each generation and is passed down from one to the next. Interaction brings issues to the surface and helps both sides face these issues.

Along with ending the occupation, the teaching of tolerance is perhaps the most important tool for achieving peace.

III
Joint economic zone

The Confederation's mock Parliament passed legislation to create a joint economic zone (JEZ) between Israel and Gaza. That zone would be exclusively under the auspices and control of the Confederation. To remind the reader, the Israeli Palestinian Confederation is made up of Israeli and Palestinian citizens. Those citizens represent the interests of their respective countries, Israel or Palestine, but also have a concurrent loyalty to the Confederation.

The JEZ would become a place where the common Israeli-Palestinian economy, education and culture would converge. A JEZ between Gaza and Israel would be equally accessible to the Palestinians from Gaza and the Israelis from Israel. The JEZ would ultimately contain an international airport that would serve both peoples, allowing Palestinians and Israelis to fly together to and from countries that currently are inaccessible.

This international airport would become a hub connecting several continents. In terms of geographical location, the area between Gaza and Israel is perfectly suited for an international airport as it is proximate to Europe, Asia and Africa.

A JEZ would become a viable option for Israeli and Palestinian producers and manufacturers who want to sell their goods to countries that were inaccessible to them in the past. Israeli companies, for example, would be able to fly their goods and products to Arab countries that have no formal relationship with Israel but would find it acceptable to have a relationship with the Israeli Palestinian Confederation. Palestinian companies and individuals would be able to ship to countries beyond their current reach.

The JEZ would include industry, agriculture and centers for education, perhaps even universities. Because this JEZ is neither Israeli nor Palestinian, it would be able to host students, investors and travelers who are now unable or unwilling to travel to either Israel or Palestine.

The JEZ is a great example of a benefit available through the Confederation but unattainable by the separate Israeli or Palestinian governments.

IV
Common passport

The Confederation's mock Parliament was able to pass legislation to create a common passport for Israeli and Palestinian citizens who reside in Israel, the West Bank and Gaza Strip. The legislation specifically stated that the common passport does not replace the current passports issued by the separate Israeli and Palestinian governments but rather supplements them. The passport would only be used in countries in which Israeli and Palestinian citizens are unable to utilize their own national passport.

If this legislation were to pass in the real Confederation government, it would have huge economic and personal implications for the citizens of Israel and Palestine. Businesspeople, tourists, intellectuals, educators and regular citizens who in the past were unable to travel or expand their business to other countries would now be able to do so. Those countries that have no formal relationship with Israel or Palestine may be open to a relationship with the Confederation since it is an independent entity. Both the Israeli and Palestinian governments would be delighted to have such economic opportunities for their people and would be hard pressed to veto this kind of legislation.

V
Compensation to Palestinian refugees

The Confederation's mock Parliament attempted to pass legislation to compensate the Palestinian refugees of 1948. The attempt was unsuccessful. The legislation stipulated that as a result of the 1948 war a substantial number of Palestinians were dislocated from Palestine, that they became refugees scattered all over the world, and that they have never received compensation. The legislation stipulated the creation of a $10 billion fund, which would be paid by several governments and entities to compensate those refugees. It would require that the funds be administered by the Confederation, that the state of Israel would pay $5 billion over a five-year period, and that supporting nations around the world would pay the balance.

There was substantial debate on this legislation. Some Parliament members argued that it is not possible to determine who is a real Palestinian refugee and who is not, and that the legislation would need to be better defined. Others argued that the legislation is an insult to the Palestinian refugees because they would have to give up their rights to return to their homeland. Other legislators argued that this was a practical solution to the refugee problem because the likelihood of their returning is very slim, and they should at least be compensated.

The discussions on this issue were long, vociferous and emotional. The significance is that the issue was brought to the table by an entity called the Israeli Palestinian Confederation, which proposed a solution. In the current impasse, neither the Israeli nor the Palestinian governments are capable of bringing this kind of issue to the table. The only entity that can discuss the issue openly and reach a resolution without fear of repercussions is the Confederation. The Confederation's Parliament members are elected for the purpose of dealing with such difficult issues and resolving them in a manner that is acceptable to both sides.

VI
Confederation police force

The mock Parliament introduced legislation creating a Confederation police force. This legislation passed successfully. In accordance with the

Constitution, the legislation was to create a police force that included an equal number of Israeli and Palestinians on each level. The police force was to be independent of the Israeli or Palestinian security forces, but it would work in cooperation with the separate Israeli and Palestinian authorities.

Some suggested that such a police force would infringe on the sovereignty of the separate Israeli and Palestinian governments. However, this argument was rejected since it was clear that the legislation creating the force was subject to a veto by the separate Israeli and Palestinian governments. The Confederation police force would be able to deal with issues relating to Confederation matters. It would not be free to make arrests of either Palestinians or Israelis on non-related matters.

The president of the mock Confederation argued that the police force would be common to both Israelis and Palestinians and that the fabric of its force represents the entire community of Israel and Palestine. He argued that the police force would be trained to deliver high quality professional service and would be sensitive to the needs of both Israelis and Palestinians. With respect to Jerusalem, he argued that the multinational Confederation police force would be sensitive to the religious requirements of both the Israelis and the Palestinians.

The mock Israeli prime minister wanted practical examples of what the police force would do. The mock president suggested that the Confederation police force would facilitate the operation of the joint economic zones, investigate corruption by administrators who refused to teach tolerance, and investigate allegations of intolerance and racist hate crime against Israelis or Palestinians. The police force would assist the Israelis and Palestinians in managing checkpoints between Israel and Palestine. It would guard the Parliament building and would investigate any threats against members of the Confederation. The police force would help make it possible for Jews, Muslims and Christians to pray in their holy places in Jerusalem without fear of violence.

VII
Pardon Anwat Breghit

The mock Parliament passed legislation to petition the Palestinian government to pardon Palestinian Anwat Breghit, who was found guilty of treason and of selling Palestinian land to Israelis. According to the indictment, Anwat Breghit sold property in the village of Beit Omar to Israelis from the Jewish settlement of Karmei Tzur. His sentence required the approval of the president of Palestine, Mahmoud Abbas. The court in Hebron sentenced Mr. Breghit to death by hanging.

The mock Israeli Palestinian Confederation petitioned Mr. Abbas not to approve the sentence and called on both the Israeli and the Palestinian governments to abolish all legislation that prohibits the sale of land based on national origin, religion or creed.

VIII
Improve relations with Iran

The mock Parliament also passed legislation to improve relations with Iran. In light of the numerous threats that have been exchanged between Israel and Iran, the deterioration of relationships between these two countries and the resulting implication of war, the legislation noted that any escalation of hostility or actual war between these two countries would harm the peoples of Israel, Palestine and Iran. The mock Parliament proposed a committee that would travel to Iran on a regular basis to negotiate a permanent and lasting peace with Iran. The members of the mock Parliament passed legislation to establish a Confederation embassy in Iran and to encourage Iran to send an ambassador who would establish residency in the joint economic zone. They passed legislation that the Confederation should negotiate a mutually acceptable peace agreement between Israel and Iran and develop commercial air travel and economic opportunities, as well as cultural exchanges, between Israel, Palestine and Iran.

This legislation to improve the relationship with Iran demonstrates the additional flexibility the Confederation offers over the present reality. Currently, there are no relationships between Israel and Iran. The relationships between Hamas and Iran are mostly adversarial to Israel. However, since the Confederation is comprised of both Israelis and Palestinians and does not represent the exclusive interests of Israel or Palestine, it may be able to discuss peace with the Iranians, a subject that neither Israelis nor Palestinians alone are able to broach with the Iranians.

IX
Redrawing the separation wall

The mock Parliament also passed legislation that called on Israel to redraw the wall in certain locations in order to reduce the hardship on both the Palestinian and Israeli peoples. In actuality, the Supreme Court of Israel had already ordered the Israeli government to do the same. The mock legislation maintained Israel's security needs but allowed more humane freedom of movement to Palestinians. Eventually, the Confederation could pass legislation to remove the wall entirely.

X
Liaison office between Israel and Palestine

The Confederation's mock legislators were able to pass legislation to facilitate free and uninterrupted dialogue between the governments of Israel and Palestine. Since those governments are not always in direct communication with each other, and since there is even less communication between Israel and Hamas, there must be a constantly available "facilitator" body to afford the parties ample opportunity to discuss matters without public scrutiny. They would also need such a body to facilitate exchange of information in case of emergencies.

Acting as such a body, the Confederation could maintain complete confidentiality to assure both sides that information would not leak to the public. This is important because many times the governments in question must maintain a certain public persona consistent with their image. At times they would be willing to compromise on their public stand, but only if they knew ahead of time that the other side was willing to compromise as well. Successful mediators use the technique of maintaining confidentiality to help opposing sides move forward in a negotiation without disclosing their ultimate objective. The opposing sides frequently are willing to disclose their true position to a mediator to help him or her "feel out" the other side and see if they are willing to meet at the same level. However, this works only when both sides trust the mediator. The exchange of information on a confidential basis is the most significant tool for a mediator to help opposing sides reach a resolution.

Outside facilitators such as the United States or Egypt do not necessarily have the trust of the Israeli or Palestinian governments. That is because the interests of those outside facilitators may differ from that of the Israeli and the Palestinian governments. In contrast, the Confederation is comprised of Israelis and Palestinians who share the interest of ultimately reaching and maintaining peace between their governments. There would be many occasions when the separate Israeli and Palestinian governments would have a much higher level of trust in the Confederation's liaison office than in an outside facilitator.

The legislation called for the establishment of a ministerial post especially designed to enhance and facilitate communication between all governments, entities and individuals, including the Israeli and Palestinian governments. The legislation provided that the minister should act as a confidential communicator and a facilitator between the parties. The legislation required that the information provided to the liaison minister would remain confidential unless otherwise instructed by the government that entrusted the minister with the information.

A ministerial post established specifically for the purpose of facilitating communications between the opposing parties would eventually become a permanent fixture in the relationship between the Israeli and Palestinian governments. He or she would eventually learn the patterns of behavior of all sides and would become familiar with the individual players, ultimately earning their trust. Unlike an outside mediator who would require special designation by an outside government, he or she would be located permanently in the geographic area and available at all hours of the day and night. This legislation would facilitate communication between the Israeli and Palestinian governments, which could, in turn, prevent an escalation of hostility.

XI

Converting Qalandia checkpoint to an education and commerce center

The Confederation's mock Parliament also passed legislation to convert the Qalandia checkpoint into an education and commerce center. Qalandia checkpoint is located on the main road between Ramallah and Jerusalem. It is a point that Palestinians traveling to Jerusalem must pass.

It is also a checkpoint where the Israeli army inspects most vehicles and individuals on their way to Jerusalem. Qalandia checkpoint is crowded and congested. It is a substantial obstacle to free travel. Palestinians feel resentful and humiliated going through this checkpoint. Israel maintains that the checkpoint is necessary to prevent suicide bombers.

The legislation that the mock Parliament passed would reduce the unnecessary congestion at the checkpoint without increasing the risk to Israel. This would be done by converting the entire area into an education and commercial zone for Palestinians and Israelis alike. The zone would be managed by the Confederation, but the entrances and exits would be monitored by the Israeli and Palestinian governments in cooperation with the Confederation police force. The legislation called for the expansion of the number of entrances and exits and required facilitation of a fast lane for more convenient passage of individuals who regularly travel between Israel and Ramallah, without compromising security.

The legislation further required construction in the Qalandia zone of educational and business centers, including a hospital and other peaceful projects, to facilitate commerce and communications. The area will become another joint economic zone, similar to the one suggested between Gaza and Israel.

This is another example of how an independent entity such as the Confederation turns lemons into lemonade. It is an example of how Israelis and Palestinians, instead of sitting across the table from each other trying to outsmart each other, can sit together in a spirit of generosity and open heartedness to create a symphony together. Israel's need for security would be addressed, but the need of the Palestinians to travel without unnecessary restrictions would be addressed as well.

XII

Emergency legislation to prevent the spread of H1N1 virus in Israel and Palestine

In 2009, the H1N1 flu virus was spreading from person to person and threatening the world's population. The virus knew no borders and could spread easily in areas where Israelis and Palestinians met, such as checkpoints.

Legislation by the mock Parliament called for the distribution and administration of the H1N1 influenza vaccine free of charge within Israel and Palestine to any person who desired it. The Confederation government was prepared to be the facilitator between the two governments in helping administer the vaccine.

The legislation required that the Palestinian and Israeli governments fully cooperate with the Confederation to permit free access to the people of Israel and Palestine for the purpose of administering the vaccine. The legislation mandated that the Confederation make efforts to negotiate with the international community and vaccine manufacturers for the purpose of obtaining the vaccine free of charge or at low cost.

The legislation further required that in the event the Confederation was unable to provide the vaccine free of charge, the governments of Israel and Palestine should reimburse the Confederation for the actual costs incurred by the Confederation. The reimbursement would be made in direct proportion to the number of citizens of each government who received the vaccine.

Many of the members of the mock Parliament praised this legislation as a prime example of the need for a confederation. At present, there is no mechanism to facilitate cooperation in case of such a threat or actual emergency. The Confederation could be the permanent facilitator of emergency help in cases of mass disaster.

XIII

Construction of a high-speed train connecting Israel and Palestine

Once the Confederation's mock Parliament had passed legislation to build an international airport in the joint economic zone between Israel and Gaza, it was necessary to continue the momentum by ensuring the economic development of the region. There was the need to provide good transportation for Palestinians and Israelis to travel to and from the joint economic zone and the airport in the fastest and most economical way.

The legislation required the installation of a high-speed train connecting the port of Haifa in northern Israel to Jerusalem and to the joint economic zone. The railroad lines would go through the entire state of Israel and the West Bank and Gaza to convey people to the international airport and the joint economic zone. The legislation called for the Confederation to obtain funding from private or public sources for the construction of the railroad, provided the list of contributors was approved by the Palestinian and Israeli governments. It required the two governments to do their utmost to assist in the construction and to refrain from interfering with the safe operation of the railroad. The legislation required that the Confederation cooperate with the Israeli and Palestinian governments to ensure that the railroad system would not pose threats to the security of the people of Israel and Palestine.

This legislation passed easily, and neither government vetoed it because they realized the tremendous implication that it would have for the economic benefit of their people.

XIV
Final-eight soccer competition

Soccer is the national game of both the Palestinian and Israeli peoples. It is also a game loved by a large segment of the world's population. Mixing sports and politics is not a new phenomenon, and when done right it can motivate and inspire.

The mock Parliament proposed a soccer tournament that combines Israelis and Palestinians on teams competing for a valuable prize. For the first time, Palestinians and Israelis would be rooting for teams based not on nationality but rather on individual players, regardless of nationality. The players on the four best Israeli and four best Palestinian teams would be randomly mixed so that each team would have an equal number of Palestinian and Israeli players. These mixed teams would compete for the championship. All participating teams would receive substantial monetary compensation, depending on their level of success. The legislation required that the Confederation solicit donors worldwide to contribute funds for this purpose.

Again, this legislation passed easily and received no veto.

XV
Improving construction standards in Palestine and Israel

The next legislation passed by the mock Parliament dealt with construction standards in Palestine and Israel. This legislation came about after the earthquake in Haiti, when it was discovered that many collapsed buildings would have survived if they had been built with proper engineering standards.

In Haiti, structures were built on slopes without proper foundations or containments, using improper building practices, insufficient steel and insufficient attention to development controls.

Due to the substandard construction, many buildings collapsed, causing devastation and the deaths of thousands of people. Much of the construction in Israel and Palestine is substandard and does not meet criteria for withstanding a severe earthquake. Similar shaking in Israel and Palestine could have equally devastating consequences.

Legislation by the mock Parliament required the establishment of a task force to improve construction standards in Israel and Palestine. The task force would review current standards and make recommendations to enhance existing criteria. The legislation provides that the task force would draft strict building codes based on acceptable engineering standards and that the Confederation would have legal authority to enforce those codes in areas where neither Israeli nor Palestinian laws have been enforced.

Again, this legislation passed overwhelmingly with the blessing of the Israeli, Palestinian and Hamas leaders.

XVI
Optional civil family laws

Many people in Israel and Palestine are ineligible or unwilling to receive services from their government relating to such family matters as marriage and divorce, which are currently controlled by religious laws. In many cases, religious exclusivity on those personal matters results in tragic consequences. There are numerous situations in which consenting adults are unable to marry or divorce due to religious restrictions.

The Israeli Palestinian Confederation is a secular government and therefore able to offer an alternative to those who cannot get help from either the Israeli or Palestinian governments. The mock Parliament passed legislation that enabled the Confederation to provide binding legal services relating to family law issues of marriage and divorce. The legislation would apply to those Palestinian and Israeli citizens who are either ineligible or unwilling to receive legal services relating to family matters from their own governments. The legislation also provides that the respective Israeli and Palestinian governments recognize the civil marriages and divorces performed by the Confederation. The legislation specifically stated that it would apply exclusively to personal family matters and nothing else.

This legislation also passed overwhelmingly by the mock Parliament and was not vetoed by the separate mock heads of state.

XVII
Permanent residency for humanitarian reasons

There are many individuals in Israel and Palestine without legal status. They include foreign workers who arrived in Israel or Palestine and overstayed their visa. Some are Palestinian nationals who moved from other countries or Gaza to the West Bank and remained there for years. Some of those individuals have put down roots in the community but are not eligible to enjoy legal status. Some have children who were born in Israel or Palestine; many speak fluent Hebrew or Arabic. Those individuals live in daily fear of being caught and deported by the authorities. They have no legal recourse and no path to citizenship. Many have not seen their families back in their homelands for decades. This is a human tragedy that needs to be addressed in a humanitarian way.

The Confederation's mock Parliament created legislation to grant citizenship to 10,000 people for humanitarian purposes. Those people would be citizens of the Confederation as an independent entity but not necessarily citizens of Israeli or Palestine. They would be given a special status that would allow them freedom to travel pursuant to the legislation.

This kind of legislation does not threaten Israel or Palestine with overwhelming immigration. It deals only with individuals who have lived in Israel or Palestine for many years and suffer personal tragedy because they are not able to disclose who they are despite deep roots in the community.

Again, this legislation was recognized by the mock Israeli and Palestinian leaders as humanitarian legislation for specific individuals and was approved.

XVIII
Israeli-Palestinian prisoner exchange

The mock Parliament passed legislation calling on the Israeli and Palestinian governments and Hamas leaders to exchange prisoners. It called on Israel to release within 10 days all children under the age of 18, along with 300 women, 300 men and all prisoners who have been detained for more than one year but not convicted.

It called on the Palestinian government and Hamas leadership to release within 10 days all Israeli prisoners in their custody, including Gilad Shalit, to the Israeli government. It called on Israel, the Palestinian government and Hamas to allow the United Nations and humanitarian organizations full access to prisoners under their control. It further required that the governments of Israel and Palestine allow representatives of the Confederation to visit those prisoners on a regular basis.

Again, this legislation was passed overwhelmingly by the mock Parliament and approved by the mock Israeli and the Palestinian government leaders.

This legislation would help both the Israeli and the Palestinian governments save face and would resolve a long and ugly stalemate between the Israeli and Palestinian governments on the issue of prisoners.

CHAPTER FOUR

THE TWO-STATE SOLUTION

A man walks to his doctor's office for help. He is 100 pounds overweight. He has diabetes and high blood pressure and difficulty breathing. Does it make sense for the doctor to tell the patient to run the marathon? For this patient, the "marathon solution" is the most dangerous prescription he could get. This patient is simply not in shape for the grueling challenge of running 26.2 miles.

No doctor in his right mind will prescribe this kind of exercise to this patient. Running the marathon may be a noble goal, but it is not the solution for this patient at this time. Perhaps the patient could run the marathon when his health improves and he loses weight and trains for a few years. But not when he is 100 pounds overweight with diabetes and high blood pressure.

The "two-state solution" is analogous to the "marathon solution." By definition, it requires the Israelis and Palestinians to agree on the most difficult issue first. In order to have this "solution," they must first agree to the "two states." This means that before anything else, there must first be an agreement between the Israeli and Palestinian governments on borders. The solution and the goal are identical. Unlike the Confederation, those governments do not have the luxury or the flexibility to deal with easier issues. This is because they are adversaries and must solve their main conflict before eliminating their animosity.

Resolution of minor issues is not part of their agenda since they have taken the path of the two-state solution, which requires them to deal with the most difficult issue first.

There are a variety of reasons why those governments are unable or unwilling to achieve the two-state solution. The Israeli and Palestinian governments are very nationalistic. Many of their constituents do not truly want peace and secretly hope for victory over the other side. They see the peace negotiations more as a delaying tactic than as voluntary cooperation. They know how to say the right phrases to remain at the negotiating table, but their purpose is to outmaneuver the other side. Neither side is willing to sign an agreement to define the final borders and put an end to the conflict. The two-state solution as presently pursued is a "virtual" solution. It is purposely vague on details. It is a legitimate cover for both sides to hide what they want and to emphasize what they don't want. It allows both sides to focus on the other side's position while deflecting their own responsibility. Both sides publicly claim to want the two-state solution, but at the same time they create obstacles to ensure it will never happen. The two-state solution is a negotiating tool used by both governments to force the other side to show its cards. Each hopes to pressure the other side to admit that it is not in favor of the two-state solution so their side can blame the other for the solution's demise.

The United Nations voted for the two-state solution to resolve the Israeli-Palestinian problem in 1947. To this day, the two states have not yet emerged. Why? Because neither the Israeli nor the Palestinian government truly wants a two-state solution. They spend most of their time blaming each other for the failure to create two states and little time negotiating in good faith.

Despite so many years of conflict, the Israelis and the Palestinians have not demanded and have not been given simple explanations from their leaders regarding the basic issues relevant to the two-state solution. There is a perplexing lack of public discussion about life in the two states after peace has been achieved. Even the term "peace" is left undefined. No leader describes his or her vision of peace.

Before a person undergoes surgery, he wants to know about life after the surgery. How long will the recovery be? What are the anticipated results? Will he be better off not having the surgery? Is there any alternative to surgery? Similar questions should be asked of and answered by the Israeli and Palestinian leaders if they are truly contemplating two states: When peace comes, is my government's goal to isolate the peoples of Israel and Palestine from each other or for us to engage each other? What is better for peace, isolation or engagement? Are we thinking of isolation first, a cooling period second and engagement third? For how long will each period last? Is it more dangerous for my country to be isolated or engaged with the other? How will we be kept isolated? When the two-state solution comes about, will we have to stamp our passports to visit the other state? Will there be a wall or a fence between the two?

The Israeli and Palestinian public and their leaders are not addressing these questions. These questions could be asked even if negotiations for peace have not yet started. These questions reflect the philosophical bent of the leaders and the public and their perception of future relations between the Palestinians and Israelis. For example, the issue of whether or not Israel and Palestine intend to isolate themselves or to engage with each other in the future is not relevant to how much land each side is willing to give up for peace. The respective leaders of both sides could discuss such questions without tipping their hand regarding their ultimate bargaining position because the questions have to do with the nature of peace, not the division of land. When these questions are not being asked, and when there are no public discussions of these issues, one can be legitimately skeptical about the sincerity of the parties to actually make peace or divide the land. Lack of public discussion of these issues by both sides is strong evidence that they are not truly interested in peace by way of two states.

Many Israelis and Palestinians oppose the two-state solution. They believe that in the long run their side will eventually prevail and eliminate the other. Many on both sides see the Israeli-Palestinian conflict as a long-term struggle. Few have a vision of current peace. Neither government is able to sign an agreement now that will spell out the borders of the two states and require them to sign a waiver of any further claims.

Historically, the negotiations for two states have proved to perpetuate violence rather than bring peace. Historically, the negotiations themselves were harmful to peace, much as the "marathon solution" would be harmful to the patient who is 100 pounds overweight. The antagonistic process and the back-and-forth public speculation on what the border will be and who will give up what has aggravated hostility rather than reducing it.

Is it nevertheless worth going through the process? Many observers understand the lack of genuine commitment to achieve the two-state solution but claim the process could have a life of its own. They claim that despite the lack of commitment, the Israeli and Palestinian governments could find themselves making peace in spite of themselves.

This argument has merits. But it is important to recognize that there are extremists on both sides who simply will not let it happen. They will prevent, by all means, those governments from reaching an agreement. The moment those governments appear to be close to serious negotiation, extremists on both sides will derail the process.

The Palestinian and Israeli governments are politically weak and lack the motivation to bring the peace process to a conclusion.

The U.S. and other countries have never been successful in facilitating negotiations between Israelis and Palestinian to the point of signing a peace agreement for a two-state solution. Even if those governments were able to reach a solution for two states, what would the peace look like? Even if we assume genuine sincerity on both sides, what kind of two states would they be able to establish? Given the security and economic concerns of each side, as well as the violent past, is it likely that the two states will look like two equal states side by side?

In all likelihood, the Palestinian state will reflect a very strange looking map on the order of an abstract drawing. It may be "contiguous" but with very narrow passageways between larger pieces of land. The Palestinian state will have no free access to the Mediterranean on the west or to the state of Jordan on the east. The Palestinian state will most likely lie exclusively within the state of Israel. It will not have any exit or entry points that are not controlled by Israel. The Palestinian state will be divided into two sections, Gaza on the west and the West Bank on the east. In short, the Palestinian state will become what it is now, the West Bank and Gaza.

Israel makes it clear that a Palestinian state must not be connected to Jordan. In addition, the Israeli government insists that the West Bank portion of the Palestinian state will be divided into two areas to allow for Israeli security zones, and it insists on a complete detachment between the West Bank and Gaza. In short, the Palestinian state will be completely surrounded and divided by Israel.

The border plan proposed by President Clinton did allow a direct connection between the Palestinian state and the state of Jordan on the east, though it maintained a complete separation between the West Bank and Gaza. It appears that Prime Minister Barak accepted the Clinton plan in 2001. However, subsequent Israeli prime ministers have insisted on the original Israeli plan.

Even if the two-state solution were to be successful, it would not lead to two states that are fully sovereign and free. The problem will remain: how do Israelis and Palestinian live in peace?

The two-state-solution process is currently being pursued in a flawed manner. In a democratic campaign in which governments are attempting to achieve a major change, they typically try to obtain support by demonstrating to their constituents the benefits of the change. Rarely do governments focus on costs or detriments. This is also true in the private sector and in everyday life. If you wish to convince people to invest or change, they must see the benefit to themselves. The way the two-state solution is being pursued, Palestinians and Israelis are mostly shown the costs, not the benefits.

From the Palestinian perspective, a two-state solution means that many Palestinians will have to give up their aspiration of returning to the actual land from which they were ejected and in which some relatives still live. The two-state solution will give them only the West Bank and Gaza, which, to some extent, they already have. To the Palestinians, the two-state solution means the end of their hopes and dreams of ever returning to their homeland.

From the Israelis' point of view, the two-state solution means they would willingly create a hostile Palestinian state similar to the Gaza Strip. The Israeli public and their government believe that a Palestinian state close to the heart of Israel is dangerous to their security. From the Israeli public's point of view, it is far better to control the Palestinians in the West Bank and Gaza then to give them full autonomy in the form of a state.

It is hard for either party to become enthusiastic about the two-state solution because they only see that they give up a lot and get little, if anything, in return.

The manner in which the two-state solution is being presented to the Israeli and the Palestinian public is that it is "the only solution" available. There has been no attempt on the part of the Israeli or Palestinian governments to expand their vision of peace. No Israeli government has attempted to describe the opportunities that Israelis will have to travel to Palestine and visit that area as tourists. There is no attempt on the side of the Palestinian government to ask their people to imagine the economic benefits that peace will bring to their people. The manner in which this solution is being marketed is that it is "the only option available." This is similar to telling a diabetic patient that amputation of the legs is the only way to treat him.

The two-state solution is not a peace plan. It is a division-of-real estate plan. It is a divorce plan. It does not enhance cooperation, dialogue and interaction between the peoples of Israel and Palestine. It does not teach tolerance and understanding. It does not encourage cooperation and engagement. It does just the opposite. It enforces a false need to separate the two. It validates and perpetuates a dangerous notion that the Israelis and Palestinians are so different from each other and so diametrically opposed to each other that they cannot live together and must be separated. Instead of encouraging the parties to engage and solve their differences, the two-state solution pretends that once they are separated, all will be well.

Nothing is further from the truth. If the Palestinians and the Israelis are separated there will be fewer common threads between the two peoples. There will be less dialogue and fewer attempts to establish mutual formulas and mechanisms to resolve issues. The alternative of "solving" issues through war will become more likely. Israelis and Palestinians who want peace will find it even more difficult to connect with each other and will be increasingly isolated in their own societies. The lubricants of peace will diminish. Isolation of the two societies will perpetuate suspicion, stereotyping and animosity.

The two-state solution is a solution between governments, not people. If such a solution becomes a reality, it will enhance the power of the governments and reduce the power of their people to demand peace.

The two-state solution is a mechanical solution. It ignores the historical connection of both peoples to the land and requires the artificial pretense that they now belong to only a portion of that land. It ignores the huge economic connections Israelis and Palestinians have with each other on a day-to-day basis in terms of commerce, roads and utility grids. It ignores the fact that Israelis and Palestinians are interwoven with each other and have families on both sides of the two states.

A Confederation government could provide an alternative. It could provide the necessary process to reach a solution. The solution should not be predetermined; it should be the product of engagement. Palestinian and Israeli members of Parliament sitting down as equals on a daily basis could certainly create the process necessary to build trust. The Parliament members will explore common ground that will not offend the Israeli and Palestinian governments. The process will be mundane and intricate. It will be slow and meticulous. But it will be a process.

The Confederation will not preclude the existing governments from pursuing their solution. It will only provide for an alternative method. Using the metaphor of health, the Confederation is the eat-well-and-exercise aspect of maintaining and enhancing health. It does not preclude the conventional methods of surgery and medication, but those conventional methods would achieve better results if the patient ate well and exercised. With a good diet and exercise, it might even be possible to eliminate the need for those conventional methods altogether, and certainly no doctor will recommend that a patient ignore his eating habits and daily exercise. The current method of solving the Israeli-Palestinian conflict lacks an alternative. The Confederation will provide this alternative.

ABOVE: *My sister Ariela, who as a teenager was saved by Arab fishermen from certain drowning in the Mediterranean. She now has three children and four grandchildren and resides in Israel.*

ABOVE: *My mother and father (on left) when they were newly engaged. My mother is 16; my father, 26. They immigrated to Palestine in 1936. Immediately upon her arrival, my mother wanted to return to Iraq because life in Palestine was too difficult, and she missed her family. She went back to Baghdad and stayed for one month but then returned to Palestine. My parents lived in Israel for over 60 years and are buried there, next to each other.*

ABOVE: *Myself in the West Bank. This photo was taken approximately three years after the 1967 war.*

ABOVE LEFT: *My father (second from left) standing near a boat next to the Euphrates River in Fallujah, Iraq, where he was born. The bridge in the background was built by the British Army. My father worked for the British Army and Air Force in Iraq and, later, in Palestine. He spoke fluent Arabic, Hebrew and English.*

ABOVE RIGHT: *My paternal grandfather David Agababa with his second wife. He had two wives at the same time, but his first wife (my grandmother) was not willing to live with him and the younger wife, so she left him. He lived most of his life in Iraq but immigrated to Israel in the 1950s after the state of Israel was established. In the Iraq of that time, many Jews and Muslims dressed in traditional Arab clothing. The two religious groups had good relationships with each other for hundreds of years.*

LEFT: *My maternal grandparents Masoda and David Hakak. They spoke only Arabic and lived in Iraq most of their lives, arriving in Israel in the 1950s only after the establishment of that state. My grandfather owned a bicycle and sewing machine sales and repair shop in Baghdad for many years. I remember that my grandmother constantly wanted to feed and kiss me.*

ABOVE: *This photo was taken around 2008 during one of my visits to the West Bank. The separation wall is a monument to the deterioration of the relationship between Israelis and Palestinians.*

CHAPTER FIVE

THE ONE-STATE SOLUTION

Those who envision the possibility of a one-state solution generally contemplate that the entire area—Israel, the West Bank and Gaza—would become one secular state under one government. While I have not seen a plan or a draft constitution that lays out the specifics, in its purest form, this vision is modeled on the many countries that separate government and religion but nevertheless allow freedom of religion. Proponents of the one-state solution envision a secular state with a body of immigration laws based on equality and objective criteria, not on religion.

It may be that the one-state solution could provide greater protection and freedom for all religions and that it might even recognize the special connections to the land claimed by Jews, Muslims and Christians. It may be that the one-state solution could bring peace and prosperity to the region. One could argue that the one-state solution is the only true democratic solution, that it would not require the removal of the Israeli settlements, and that it would permit free and uninterrupted access to religious sites. In a vacuum, the one-state solution makes sense. However, this solution is the least likely to be accepted in the foreseeable future.

Most Israeli Jews, and perhaps some Palestinians, do not want to have a secular state precisely because it is secular. This is despite the fact that most are themselves secular. The majority of Jews in Israel and many people around the world believe in the idea of Zionism. They are convinced that Israel is the homeland for the Jewish people, that the Jewish people endured anti-Semitism for centuries and suffered the Holocaust and that they are therefore entitled to their own state for their own protection. This notion is so engrained in most Israeli Jews that any argument to the contrary falls on deaf ears.

Any attempt to create a one-state solution is seen by Israel as an attempt to destroy the state of Israel. From the Jewish perspective, one state means the annihilation of everything the Jews were finally able to accomplish by having their own homeland. At this time, any realistic person will have to agree that any formula for peace must include a separate state for the Jews called Israel.

Contradicting Israel's position against a one-state solution is its inability to extract itself from the Palestinians. Israel wants to be in control of the Palestinians but is unwilling to offer them Israeli citizenship. Israel is unable to come up with a solution and is trying to have its cake and eat it too. The government of Israel simply does not have the tools, the imagination or the political will to make up its mind. If Israel objects to the idea of one state, it must resolve the occupation. If Israel wants to maintain the occupation, it must give full citizenship rights to the Palestinians.

Given the current spirit of democracy and the tremendous awakening in the Arab world, it is doubtful that the majority of Palestinians will be willing to remain silent in a state-within-a-state that offers them limited rights and opportunities.

The Palestinians currently have limited political and military power in comparison to Israel. They are capable of inflicting harm on Israel, but not a fatal blow. Most Palestinians are looking to live in peace and to seek equality. Many Palestinian intellectuals prefer the one-state solution, although the Palestinian government and Hamas do not seem to be enthusiastic about this idea.

In 2008, I attended a panel discussion in Santa Monica, California. Two of the speakers, U.C.L.A. professor Saree Makdisi and Ghada Karmi, a Palestinian doctor who frequently writes on this issue, were of the opinion that the only option for peace between Palestinians and Israelis is the one-state solution. Under this solution, there will be no "Palestinian government" and no "Israeli government" but rather one government, pluralistic in nature, for the entire population. When the two speakers were asked if such a solution is practical in light of strong objections from the Israeli population, their response, in essence, was that one must strive for the best and most just solution and not compromise one's principles for practical considerations.

In a conversation I had with Jewish-American activist Anna Baltzer, who also favors the one-state solution, she rejected the idea of a confederation on the grounds that it is similar to the separate-but-equal doctrine that justified a system of segregation in the United States. Services, facilities and public accommodations were allowed to be separated by race on the condition that the quality of each group's public facilities was to remain equal. In 1954, however, the U.S. Supreme Court reversed this doctrine, holding that "separate but equal" has no place in a civil society desiring equality. Separate educational facilities, the court held, are inherently unequal. Ms. Baltzer argued that the Confederation government suggested in this book endorses the separate-but-equal doctrine in the context of the Israeli-Palestinian conflict.

Ms. Baltzar is mistaken. The Israeli Palestinian Confederation Constitution does not allude to any separate-but-equal doctrine. In fact, the opposite is true; the Constitution clearly applies to both the Israelis and the Palestinians as equals. It provides for equal sharing of power and equal representation in all branches of governments. There is not one instance in which it provides any preferential treatment or unequal treatment for either nationality or religion.

Ms. Baltzer will argue that the Confederation supports the continued existence of the governments of Israel and Palestine and by doing so endorses the continued separation between the Palestinians and the Israelis.

The Confederation Constitution does not exclude or include the idea of a one-state solution. The preamble of the Constitution states in part, "The Israeli Palestinian Confederation does not intend to supersede or supplant the Palestinian or Israeli governments, nor to abrogate or undermine any agreements between those governments."

Should the separate Israeli and Palestinian governments agree on a one-state solution, the Confederation is not constitutionally able to stand in the way. But such an agreement in the foreseeable future is highly unlikely. It appears that for the foreseeable future, the only way to achieve "one state" is to remove those governments and their military powers. The question then becomes: How does one remove the Israeli government, the Hamas government and the PLO government?

Some Israelis have their own vision of a one-state solution. Their vision is for the entire area, including Israel, the West Bank and Gaza, to comprise the state of Israel. The Palestinians in those areas would be relocated or transferred to other Arab nations, and the Palestinian population would be replaced by Israelis. Their "one state" would be the state of Israel.

Ironically, I find that both the Israeli and Palestinian versions of the one-state solution have similarly unrealistic expectations. The Palestinian version requires that the current Israeli, Hamas and PLO governments dissolve themselves, since one cannot have a "one state" that will be controlled by the Israeli or Palestinian governments. As a precondition for the creation of the one state, both the Israeli and the Palestinian governments will need to be eliminated.

According to numerous sources, including the Central Bureau of Statistics of both Israel and Palestine, *Time* magazine and various atlases, it appears that as of 2008, the total Palestinian population in the West Bank, East Jerusalem and the Gaza Strip was approximately 4 million. In addition, there were 1.5 million Arabs who were citizens of Israel. The likelihood that they will voluntarily relocate to other Arab states is nonexistent. Theoretically, the only way to remove or transfer them is by force. No Israeli government has been or will be willing to do so. Even if we put aside the practical and moral problems involved with transferring Palestinians to other countries, it is clear that such an outcome could come about only by force. Clearly, the Palestinian and Israeli proponents of the one-state solution are proposing some sort of violence to achieve their version of the solution.

But no one has yet been able to destroy the governments of Palestinians and Israel. No one has the means or desire to do so in the future. No one has been able to transfer the Palestinians from the West Bank and Gaza, and no credible force in the area has the means or desire to do so in the future.

Even assuming arguendo that at some future date a one-state solution is conceivable, what is the plan for peace between the Palestinians and the Israelis until that single state is established? If that one state isn't established for another 50 or 100 years, what are the plans for the meantime? Do its proponents expect the two sides to continue to harass each other until the day the one state is established?

These questions bring me back to the marathon metaphor I like to use. Is it responsible for a doctor to prescribe the ultimate goal of running the marathon to his patient as the only goal? Is it responsible for a doctor to tell his overweight, diabetic, high-blood-pressure patient not to bother improving his diet and exercising unless he intends to run the marathon? Is an 85 percent improvement not worth trying just because it is not 100 percent?

I believe that such a position negates practical reality. There is never a 100 percent solution to any social or political issue. Almost nothing in life is 100 percent accomplished. We do not live our lives that way.

This reminds me of a conversation I had with Stephen Mashney, a Palestinian-American lawyer. I presented him with the idea of the Confederation and sensed his unwillingness to accept this proposal. I pointed out our common profession and argued that based on our mutual experiences, most legal cases eventually settle. I suggested that we should consider the merits of a confederation as a mechanism of settling the Israeli-Palestinian conflict. Mr. Mashney said my problem was that I thought like a lawyer. He explained that as lawyers, we think in terms of finality. Every legal case is on a path to trial. The parties must assess their respective positions in light of the finality that the trial represents. If they do not settle, they eventually have to present their case to a judge or a jury for a final decision.

According to Mr. Mashney, the Israeli-Palestinian conflict will never come to trial and will never be decided by a judge or jury and therefore has no finality. Mr. Mashney's opinion was that the Israeli-Palestinian conflict does not have to be resolved in his lifetime, that it is a long-term conflict that could last centuries, and that the Palestinians will win because their birthrate is much higher than the Israeli birthrate, and by sheer numbers they will eventually control the area. Mr. Mashney opined that eventually Israel would not be able to control a Palestinian population much larger than its own. He further stated that unlike the Israelis who like to live in luxury and need the good life, Palestinians could survive rugged conditions and will be able to outlast them.

In my opinion, one cannot make sweeping conclusions that the Palestinians will eventually win because the Israelis are too spoiled to fight them for 100 years or because they will outnumber the Israelis. At the same time, it is impossible to theorize that Israel will win because it will always maintain military and technological superiority over the Palestinians. Survival is the strongest instinct of human nature. The likelihood that a whole nation of people will agree to go down without a fight is unrealistic. Even if the Israelis become too spoiled, they will not give up easily when it comes to their survival, and even if the Palestinians are not as technologically advanced, they will find ways to fight the Israelis on their terms.

Another perspective on the one-state solution came from Daniel Pipes, who expressed his belief that peace will come to the area only after one side prevails over the other.

I disagree with the analysis by Stephen Mashney and Daniel Pipes that there is only one way to solve the conflict. They both believe that peaceful resolution of the conflict by way of a political process is out of the question. Their prediction is borrowed from historical analyses explaining the demise of empires or superpowers that collapsed when they were unable to project military or economic power.

Both Mr. Mashney and Mr. Pipes are missing the point. Peace needs to come now, and we must make it happen. It is irresponsible to abrogate our current responsibilities to resolve the conflict in favor of unproven theories. Even if they are correct, we should do our utmost to change the "eventual outcome" by introducing a new formula in an effort to achieve peace. Achieving peace by winning or destroying the other side is an inferior and much less desirable method than achieving peace through a political process.

We have been able to make tremendous strides in fighting cancer, diabetes and other diseases that in the past were considered deadly. We have been able to reach technological heights never imagined before. We have been able to improve world communication and travel in ways not imaginable 20 years or even a decade ago. We have been able to bring down autocratic governments in Europe and the Middle East in ways not imagined before. There is no reason why we cannot confront the last frontier, the Israeli-Palestinian conflict, in a way that has not been attempted before.

The last 30 years have given us unbelievable improvements in communication and created a platform for change not previously available, either to empires or superpowers. We now connect with people across the street and around the globe with the same ease and speed. We now communicate with people who are citizens of countries with whom our governments maintain little or no connection. We now form social networks and realize that we share the same views despite differences in our national identity or religion. We are now more sophisticated and do not view issues in the same single dimension as we have in the past. This change is permanent and irreversible. We are much more educated and open to scrutinizing our governments, and we have better methods to challenge them. In short, we live in a completely different era. We have excellent tools, both technological and intellectual, to tackle the Israeli-Palestinian conflict. We should take full advantage of all this.

We therefore return to the theme of this book. Since their own governments are not able to offer peace to Palestinians and Israelis, the people should do it on their own. An independent government representing the interests of both the people of Israel and of Palestine makes much sense.

The Israeli Palestinian Confederation Constitution provides a practical alternative to the one-state solution.

The Constitution focuses on people, not on land. It confers rights and duties to the people regardless of where they live and how their government behaves. The Confederation does not preclude any other alternative, but it recognizes that despite decades of hostility, the separate governments of Israel and Palestine have not been able to agree on a formula for peace.

The Confederation will not be able to dictate any solution that is not acceptable to the separate governments of Israel and Palestine. Article I, Section 2 of the Confederation Constitution states, "No bill shall become law unless 55 percent of the Palestinian and 55 percent of the Israeli members of Parliament have passed it, and unless the respective Israeli and Palestinian heads of governments and the separate Israeli and Palestinian legislative bodies have been given a reasonable and equal opportunity to veto said bill, and unless said governments and legislative bodies decline to veto such legislation within a reasonable time as prescribed by the bill."

Because the Parliament is comprised of citizens of Israel and Palestine and must have a supermajority of both Israelis and Palestinians before it reaches consensus, the likelihood of any side running roughshod over the other or taking advantage of the other is greatly reduced.

In addition, the Constitution provides one more safeguard to protect the interests of the Israeli and Palestinian governments. According to the Constitution, any legislation passed by the Parliament could be vetoed by the executive or legislative branch of each separate government.

All these safeguards ensure that the entire political spectrum of the peoples of Israel and Palestine could refuse any legislation passed by the Confederation Parliament.

After so many decades of failure in the Israeli-Palestinian peacemaking business, it is irresponsible for any person to suggest that an Israeli Palestinian Confederation is not worth pursuing because it is not 100 percent.

CHAPTER SIX

Could the U.S. Impose Peace?

Many have suggested that the United States is the only party in the world that could impose peace between the Palestinians and the Israelis. The thinking behind this theory is that the Palestinians are so weak militarily, politically and economically that they are no match for the Israelis at the bargaining table or on the battlefield, and therefore they will not be able to strike a fair deal with Israel. Without a fair deal for the Palestinians, no realistic agreement can be reached, so the thinking is that since the U.S. is the only party that Israel will respect, the U.S. should impose a deal on the Israelis. The conventional wisdom is that Israel is dependent on the U.S. for military aid and political support, and that it cannot afford to lose this support, and therefore the U.S. can exert pressure on Israel to accept reasonable conditions for peace.

Many countries, including the U.S., have attempted numerous times to negotiate peace between the Israelis and the Palestinians, all without success. Many organizations and private and public individuals have done the same with similar results.

The U.S. has the largest economy in the world, but that economy is dependent on the uninterrupted flow of oil. Indeed, the whole world's economy is dependent on oil. The U.S. has a vital interest in Middle Eastern oil flowing without interruption. It has huge economic and strategic interests in the region, far beyond the limited geography of Israel and Palestine.

The flow of oil from the Middle East to the rest of the world was interrupted after the 1967 and the 1973 wars between Israel and its Arab neighbors. After these wars, the U.S. realized that the region is not only rich in oil but also rich in controversies and disputes. These disputes range from the Israeli-Palestinian conflict to the Israeli-Arab conflict to internal conflicts within the ruling autocracies in the Middle East. The U.S. believes that in order to maintain the flow of oil from the Middle East, it must maintain stability and prevent any uncontrolled eruptions of war in the region.

Until 1967, Israel received most of its military support from France. Before that, the U.S. was not a strong supporter of Israel because it was not willing to jeopardize its relations with the Arabs. As a result of the 1967 war, however, the U.S. realized that Israel was strong militarily and had the ability to destabilize the Middle East. In order to maintain stability between Israel and its Arab neighbors and to have better leverage over Israel, the U.S. saw that it had to offer its support to Israel.

What will happen if the U.S. withdraws that support? Will Israel change its policy toward the Palestinians? The U.S. knows that abandoning Israel will create huge instability in the Middle East. Should the U.S. decide to abandon it, Israel will immediately seek (and easily find) other world powers that will be willing to replace the U.S. in that area. The U.S. will gain nothing by abandoning Israel. It will prove itself an unreliable ally and will lose leverage over the Arab countries as well. The U.S. must maintain its special relationship with Israel to be able to have a measure of control over it.

Should the U.S. abandon Israel, it will never be able to reassert control. The Israelis will see this abandonment as a threat to their existence and be extra motivated to find other means to expand its security and national interests.

Israel's willingness to allow the U.S. some measure of control over its conduct does not come without a price, but Israel understands that it has leverage over the U.S. as well. Israel's leverage stems from its proximity to the world's most important oil resources and its own huge military powers, which are capable of threatening the whole world's economy and safety. Israel further understands that the U.S. is using the special U.S.-Israeli relationship as leverage over the Arab nations. Israel understands that it is a vital interest of the U.S. to maintain stable relationships with all the countries of the Middle East and that the U.S. is willing to pay a hefty price to maintain that stability. Israel understands that it has the capability of undermining that stability and that the U.S. is willing to go a long way to prevent her from doing so.

The internal division between the White House and Congress regarding the Israeli-Palestinian conflict and many other issues in the Middle East makes the Americans' ability to pressure the parties even more tenuous. The Israeli and Palestinian lobbyists in Congress and their public relations efforts to influence American opinion add to the confusion. There is no decisive and clear view in the U.S. on how the peace between Israel and Palestine should be achieved. As a result, the U.S. government does not have strong support from the American people to impose peace. This makes the U.S. government even weaker in the region.

Toward the last months of his administration, President Clinton made a huge personal commitment and used every means at his disposal to convince the Israelis and Palestinians to reach an agreement through a two-state solution. Despite his intense efforts and personal charm coupled with the full power and strength of the U.S. government, the negotiations failed. As Dennis Ross wrote in his 2004 book *The Missing Peace*, President Clinton's proposal appeared reasonable to any objective observer. It was later disclosed that it was Yasser Arafat who rejected the deal, but it is not completely clear that Prime Minister Barak accepted it nor that the Israeli government would have approved it.

As a result of the failed negotiations between Clinton, Barak and Arafat, the Palestinians have lost much political power and Israel seems to have gained more. However, the U.S. role as a capable broker was diminished because it was unable to deliver an agreement. It became clear that the formula of the two-state solution proposed by President Clinton pushed the two sides to their respective bottom lines.

Since the Clinton failure, subsequent U.S. administrations have repeated their belief that the only solution is the two-state solution. It is quite perplexing why the U.S., which has tried so hard yet failed to reach that solution, will insist on it as the "only" solution." Where exactly did President Clinton not try hard enough? What land was forgotten in those negotiations? It became abundantly clear in those negotiations that having those leaders sit together with a map and a pencil dividing towns, streets and mountain ranges does not suffice and may even be counterproductive. If anything, the two-state solution is even less likely now since both the Israelis and the Palestinians are retreating from the end point of those negotiations.

The U.S. seems to be making the same mistake made by others. It reduces the solution to a single dimension, which is the division of real estate. It is astonishing that despite the decreased chances for a two-state solution, the U.S. does not pursue other innovative solutions, such as a confederation. Even if the U.S. decides to exert pressure on the parties, the most it will be able to reach is an agreement. It will not be able to dictate peace. The U.S. should make a dramatic change in its policies. In addition to emphasizing stability, it should advocate peace. Should the U.S. demand and expect peace, not just stability, its standing in the region will be elevated. The Israeli or Palestinian governments will not be able to oppose the U.S. if it publicly supports a confederation. Should the U.S. admit that its previous plans for a two-state solution failed, its status in the region will not suffer but rather be enhanced. Should the U.S. accept the idea that there are other means to forge peace between the Israelis and the Palestinians, its relationship with them will remain intact and probably even strengthen. Should the U.S. agree to open up the process of peace and refrain from limiting itself to a single solution, it will be viewed as an honest and sincere broker. In the long run, the U.S. will have better relationships within the region if it advocates the notion that peace between the Israelis and the Palestinians can come from them alone. The U.S. should emphasize that peace can only be earned by the parties themselves through hard work and dedication on a daily basis.

The two-state solution is an "all or nothing" approach. The premise of this approach is that until the parties agree on the division of land between them, the status quo remains the same. Albert Einstein's definition of insanity—doing the same thing over and over again and expecting different results—is quite fitting in this context. This kind of "all or nothing" approach is also uncharacteristic of the U.S.; most Americans are trained to think in terms of options and alternatives. As the country with the most influence in the region, the U.S. simply cannot afford to be limited by a single option or by stagnation of thinking.

The U.S. role in creating peace between the Israelis and the Palestinians should be global rather than intricate. The U.S. should not be sitting with a map and a pencil divvying up streets and blocks. It should not be under the hood changing oil or fixing the engine. It should be in the executive office viewing different ideas for peace. Instead of bogging itself down with the details, it should take a broader approach as a facilitator of peace rather than a negotiator for peace. It should facilitate peace in the same manner that the National Institutes of Health facilitates medical care, not by wielding a stethoscope on individual patients, but by enabling scientific research.

The U.S., or for that matter any other country, should not conduct its peace efforts the same way it conducts its war efforts. War is the opposite of peace. A successful war operation requires working with the army and with intelligence agencies. It requires secrecy and surprise. Most of the time civilians are not part of wars and do not participate in them. Peace should be conducted in a different way. It should not be made in secret; it should involve as many people as possible. It should be transparent and predictable. The public should participate in the peace process and should demand to understand the process and contribute to it.

The U.S. should lead the way. It has the resources and the vision to open up the peace process. Its vital interests and standing in the region will be greatly enhanced if it does so.

Maps of the Region

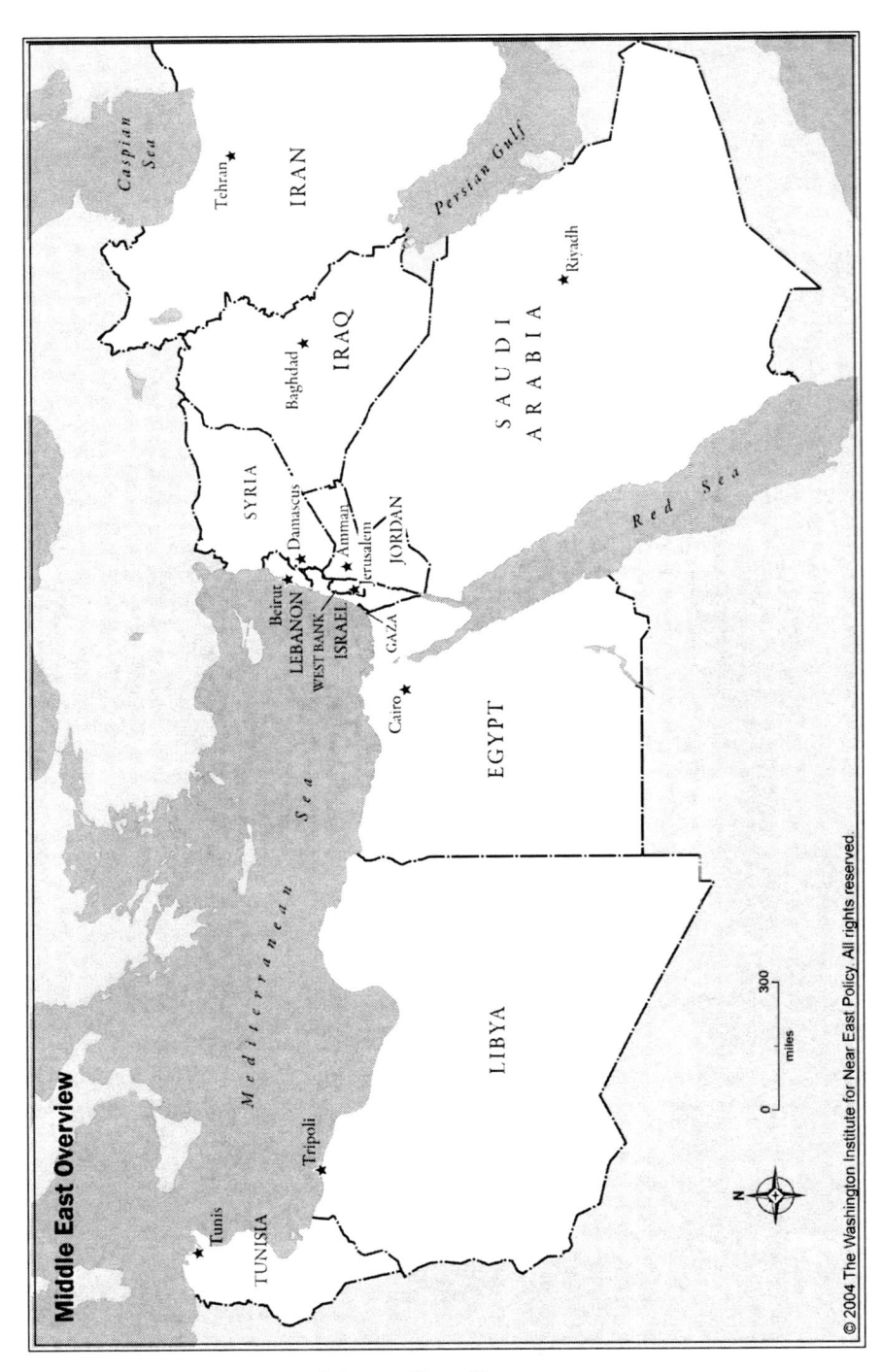

MIDDLE EAST OVERVIEW

MAP I

MIDDLE EAST OVERVIEW

An overview of the region shows how central Israel and Palestine are to Europe, Africa and Asia. Many of the countries shown in this map have no diplomatic relationships with either the Israelis or the Palestinians. As a neutral entity, the Israeli Palestinian Confederation may be able to establish ties with some of them. A joint economic zone between Gaza and Israel is an ideal location for an international airport that would connect three continents and have a significant positive economic effect on the region.

Copyright ©2004 Washington Institute for Near East Policy
Reproduced with permission.

ISRAEL, 1949 ARMISTICE

MAP 2

ISRAEL, 1949 ARMISTICE

This map shows the United Nations' 1947 partition plan. The concept of "two states" was introduced even before the creation of the state of Israel, and the "two-state solution" has been tried many times. This solution is not inconsistent with an Israeli Palestinian Confederation, but it makes sense to create a confederation now, even if the two states have not yet been delineated.

Copyright ©2004 Washington Institute for Near East Policy
Reproduced with permission.

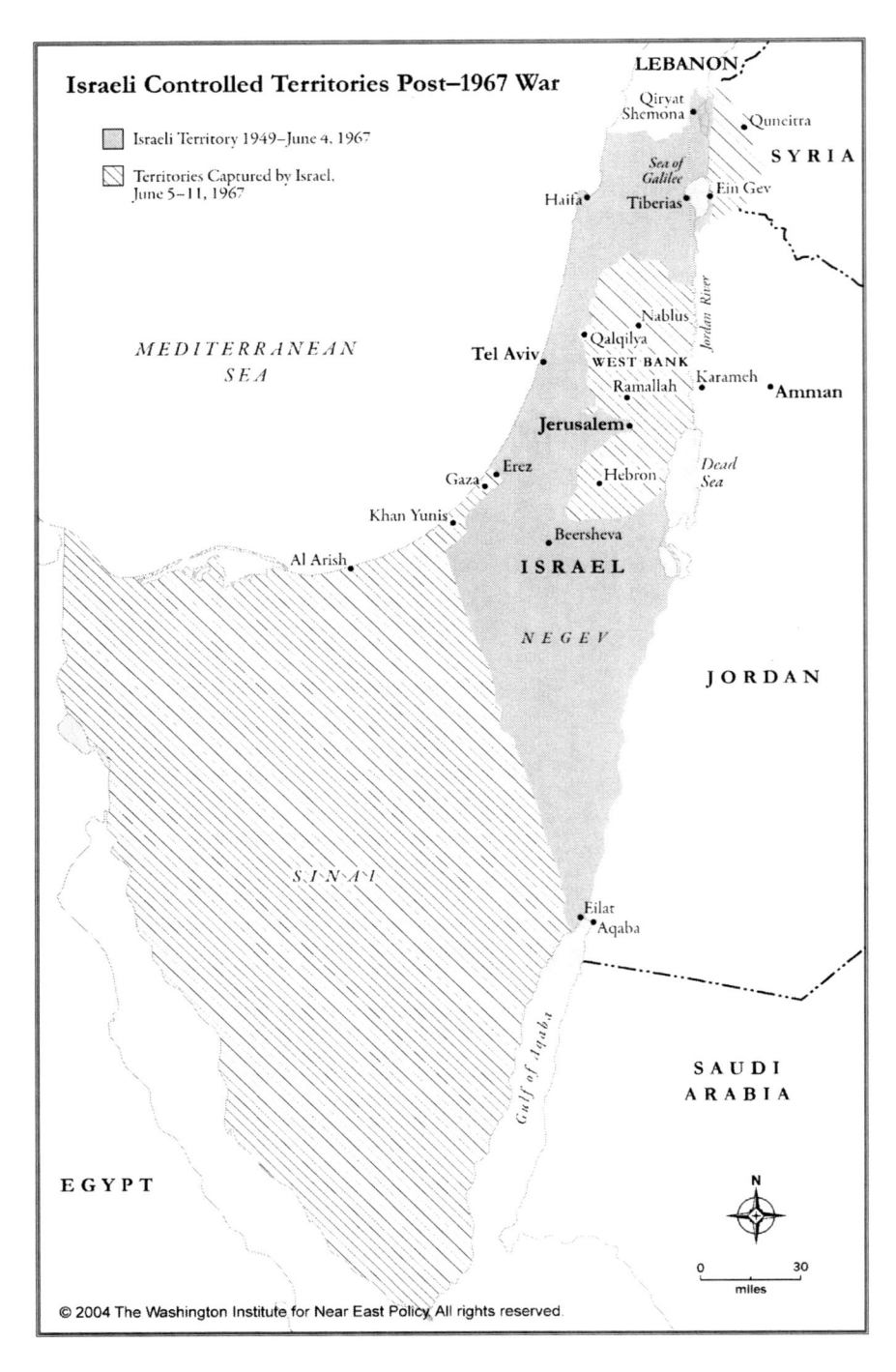

ISRAELI CONTROLLED TERRITORIES - POST 1967 WAR

MAP 3

ISRAELI CONTROLLED TERRITORIES POST 1967 WAR

This map shows the area captured by Israel during the 1967 war. The Sinai was returned to the Egyptians, but Gaza remained as a Palestinian territory. The West Bank is the area where many Israeli settlements exist. In theory, the Palestinians want the West Bank and Gaza in its entirety as part of the Palestinian state. In theory, the Israelis are willing to give some of those territories to the Palestinians; however, they want to maintain many of the settlements and security zones. Both sides are intent on keeping their true goals a secret until they agree on borders for two sovereign states. The Israeli Palestinian Confederation does not oppose an agreement for a two-state solution between the government of Israel and the government of the Palestinian people, but as a third government for all the people of Israel, the West Bank and Gaza, the Confederation could help resolve conflicts.

Copyright ©2004 Washington Institute for Near East Policy
Reproduced with permission.

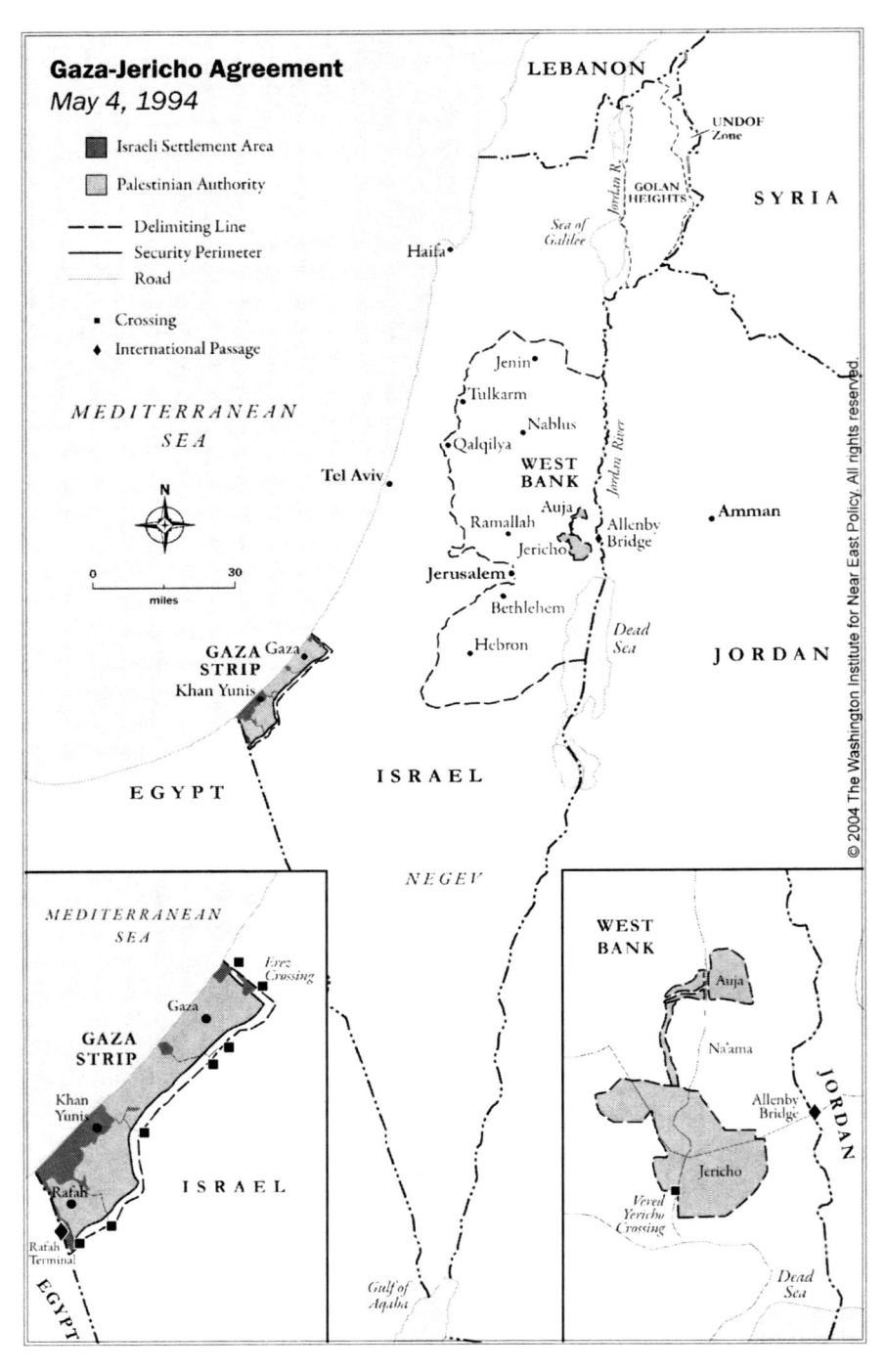

GAZA - JERICHO AGREEMENT

*Maps 4, 5, and 6, all featured in Dennis Ross'
2004 book* The Missing Peace, *chronicle the various
attempts to find a two-state solution.
They demonstrate vividly how small the area is
and how difficult it is to come up with an agreement
to end the conflict via a two-state solution.*

MAP 4

GAZA JERICHO AGREEMENT

Copyright ©2004 Washington Institute for Near East Policy
Reproduced with permission.

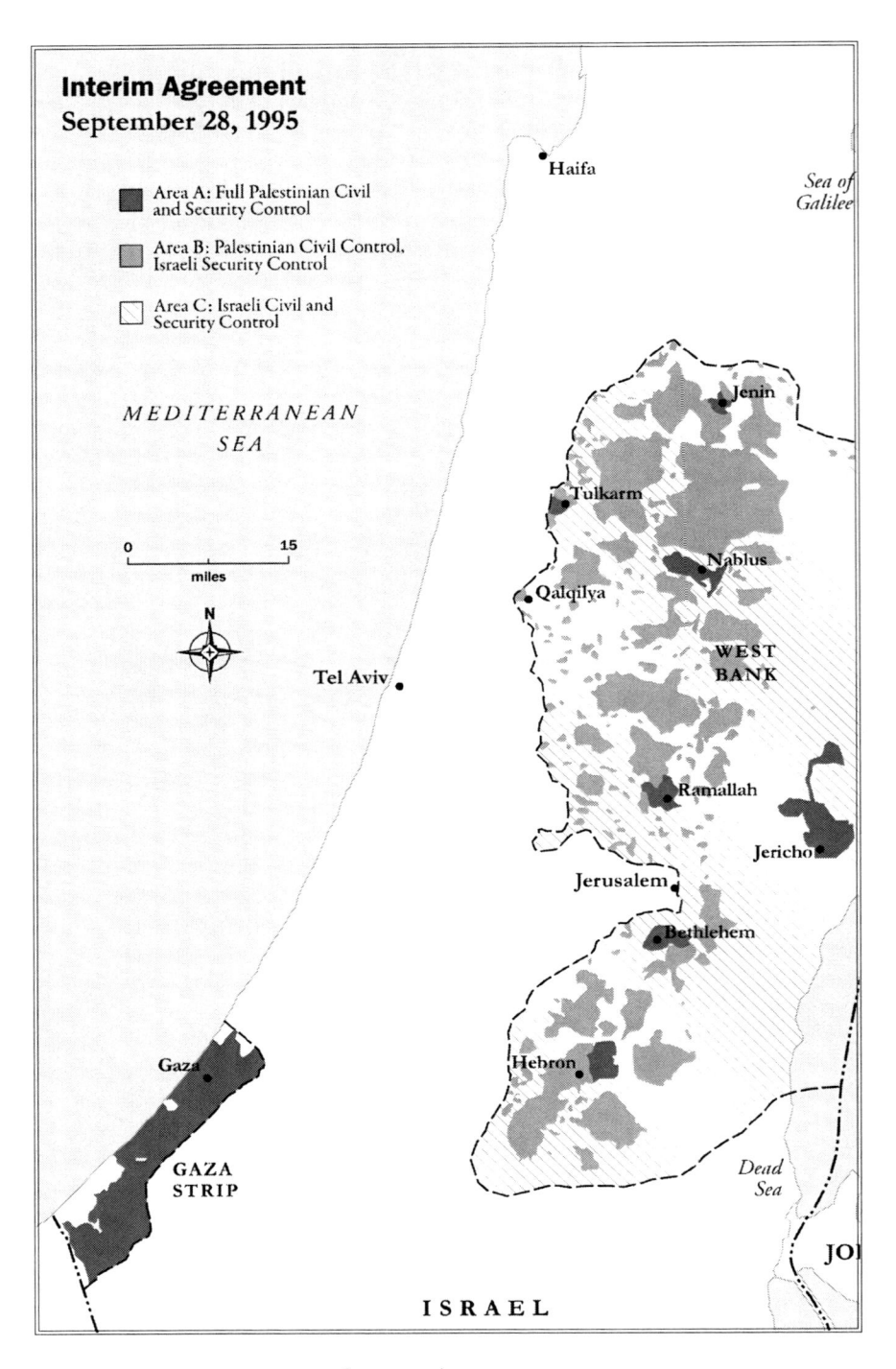

INTERIM AGREEMENT

MAP 5

INTERIM AGREEMENT

Copyright ©2004 Washington Institute for Near East Policy
Reproduced with permission.

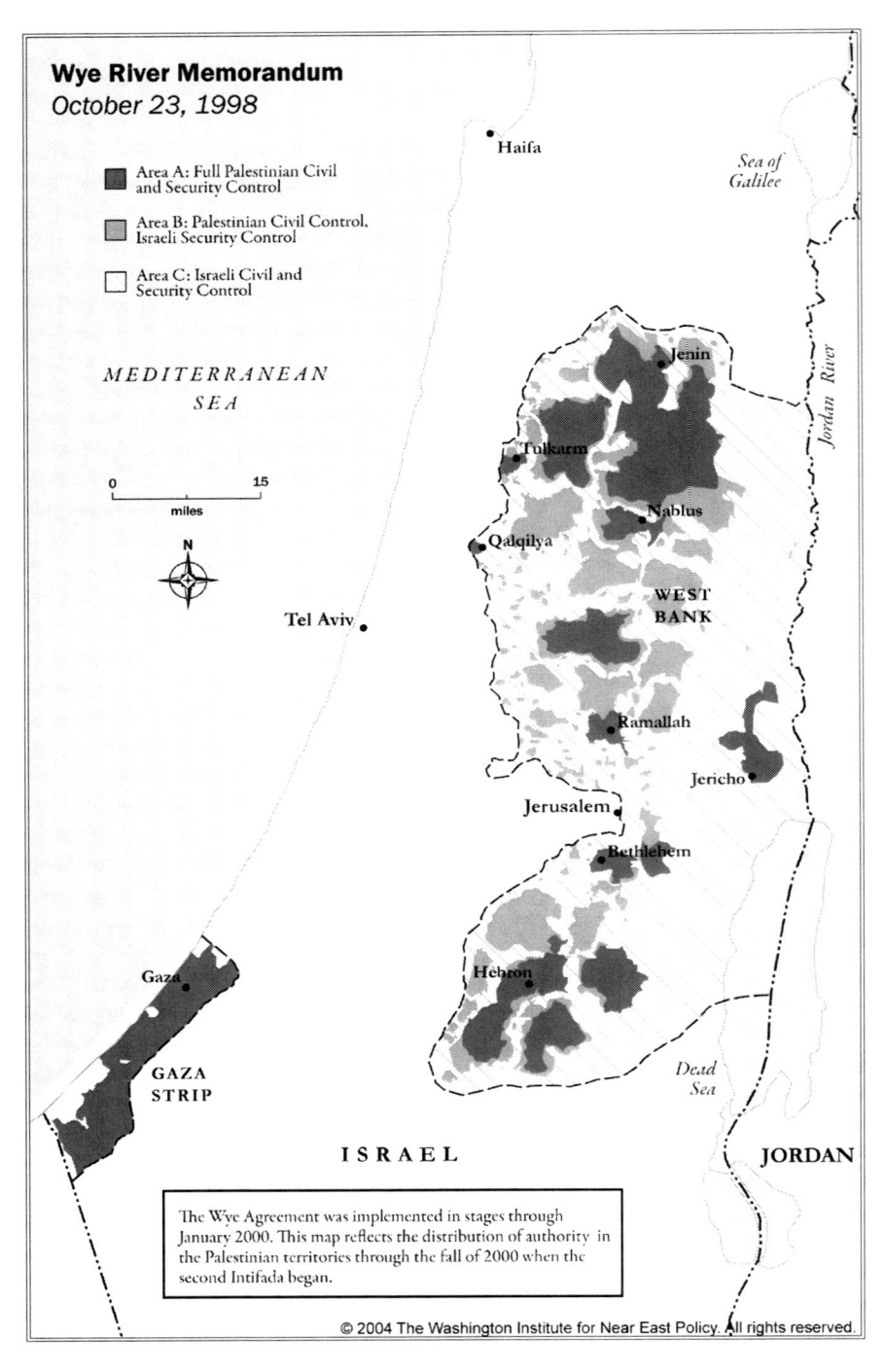

WYE RIVER MEMORANDUM, OCTOBER 23, 1998

MAP 6

WYE RIVER MEMORANDUM, OCTOBER 23, 1998

Copyright ©2004 Washington Institute for Near East Policy
Reproduced with permission.

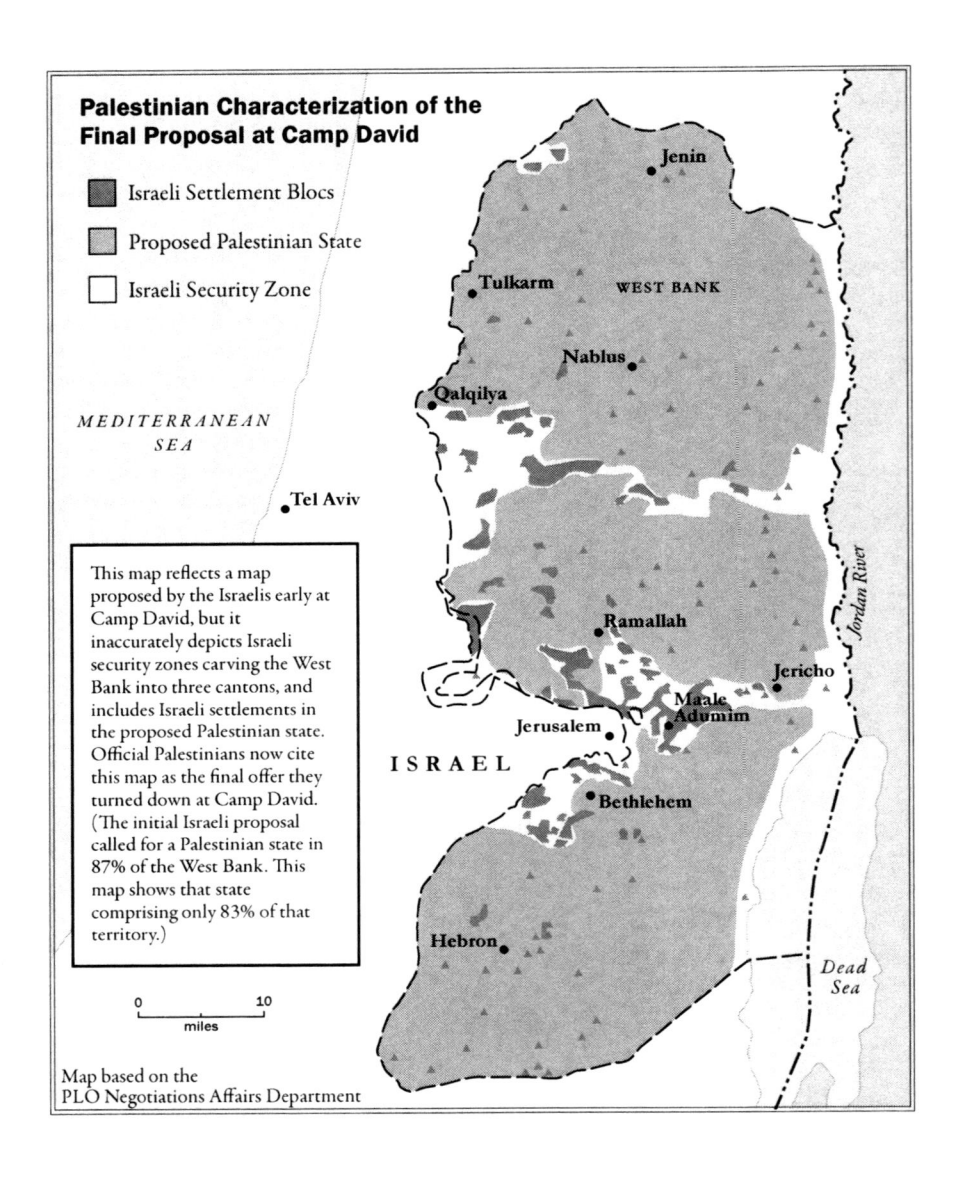

Palestinian Characterization of the Final Proposal at Camp David

- ■ Israeli Settlement Blocs
- ▨ Proposed Palestinian State
- □ Israeli Security Zone

This map reflects a map proposed by the Israelis early at Camp David, but it inaccurately depicts Israeli security zones carving the West Bank into three cantons, and includes Israeli settlements in the proposed Palestinian state. Official Palestinians now cite this map as the final offer they turned down at Camp David. (The initial Israeli proposal called for a Palestinian state in 87% of the West Bank. This map shows that state comprising only 83% of that territory.)

0 — 10 miles

Map based on the PLO Negotiations Affairs Department

PALESTINIANS CHARACTERIZATION OF THE FINAL PROPOSAL AT CAMP DAVID

MAP 7

PALESTINIAN CHARACTERIZATION OF THE FINAL PROPOSAL AT CAMP DAVID

It appears that the Israelis proposed this division early on during the failed Camp David Summit in 2000. Based on this map, the West Bank would have been split into three territories. The Palestinian state would have been a state within the state of Israel. This map clearly shows how difficult it is to create two sovereign states.

Copyright ©2004 Washington Institute for Near East Policy
Reproduced with permission.

Map Reflecting Clinton Ideas

- Proposed Palestinian State
- Israeli Settlement Blocs Annexed to Israel

No formal map was presented to the Israelis and Palestinians in December 2000 by President Clinton, but this map illustrates the Clinton ideas—a Palestinian state in 95% of the West Bank and 100% of Gaza. This map actually understates the Clinton ideas by not showing an additional 1 to 3% of territorial swaps to the Palestinian state from areas within Israel.

© 2004 The Washington Institute for Near East Policy. All rights reserved.

Map Reflecting Clinton Ideas

MAP 8

MAP REFLECTING CLINTON IDEAS

This map shows President Bill Clinton's two-state proposal, which shaves substantial area from the West Bank and splits the Palestinian state into the West Bank and Gaza. It appears that this map was rejected by Yasser Arafat during negotiations at the Camp David Summit. However, it is not clear that Ehud Barak or the Israeli government accepted this map.

Copyright ©2004 Washington Institute for Near East Policy
Reproduced with permission.

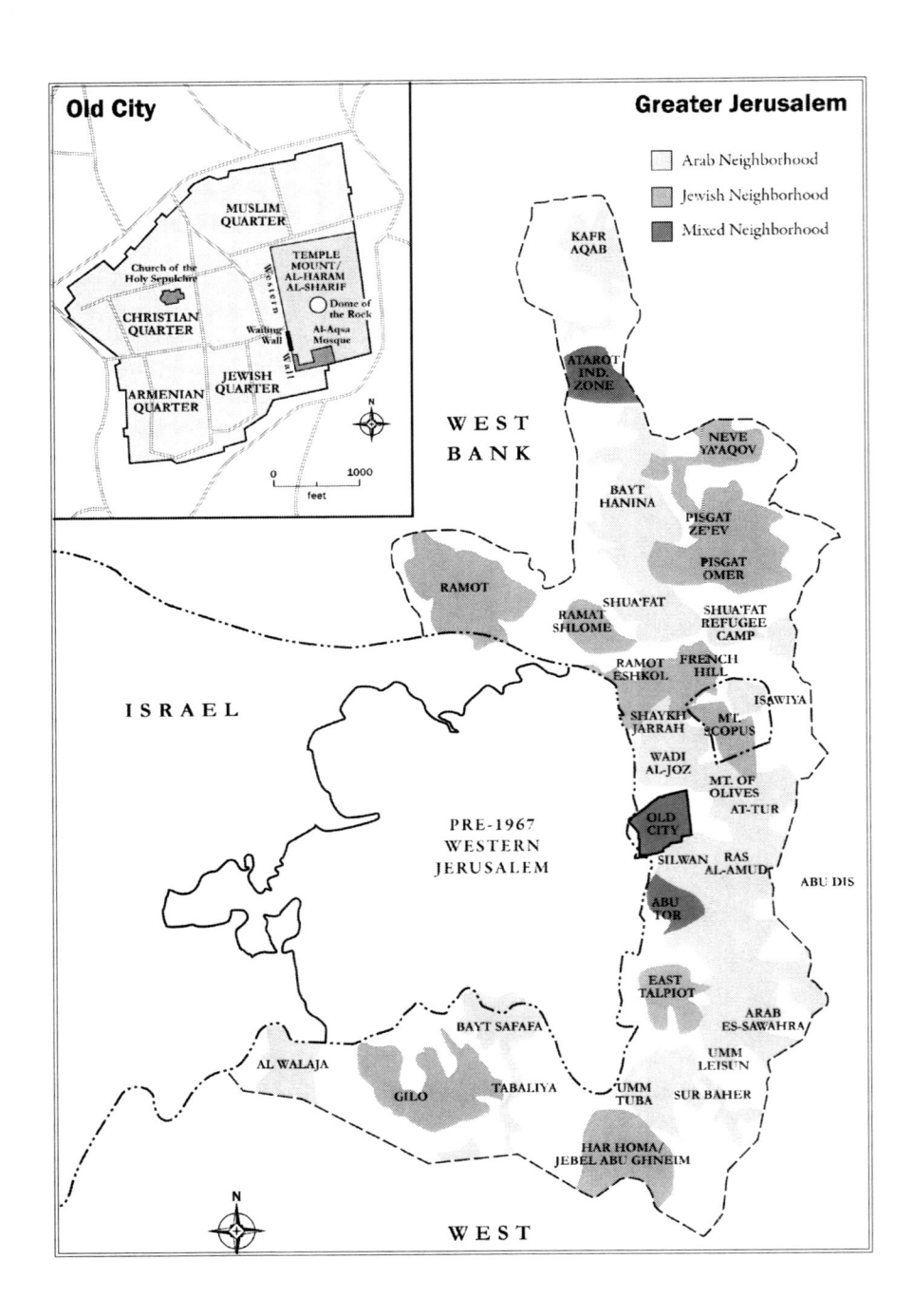

GREATER JERUSALEM

MAP 9

GREATER JERUSALEM

This map shows how close the Arab, Jewish and mixed neighborhoods are to each other. In fact, they are substantially interwoven. The map demonstrates how difficult it is to divide the area and why a confederation government makes so much sense.

Copyright ©2004 Washington Institute for Near East Policy
Reproduced with permission.

CHAPTER SEVEN

Skeptic's Corner

Currently, there are many more skeptics than supporters of the idea of an Israeli Palestinian Confederation. However, since this concept has not been tried before, none of them speak from experience. Admittedly, the Confederation's supporters have the same vantage point.

When Theodor Herzl envisioned the movement of Jews from the Diaspora after 3,000 years of exile from Palestine, most Jews were skeptics. This skepticism did not stop millions of them from all over the world from going to Palestine and Israel. Lack of prior attempt should not justify no attempt.

The blueprint for the Israeli Palestinian Confederation should be judged on its merits. The idea should be subject to rigorous questioning and should rise or fall on the quality of the answers. However, the measuring standards should include the following:

1) *Does a confederation have the potential to advance the cause of peace between the Israelis and the Palestinians?*

2) *Are there objectively better alternatives for peace between the Israelis and the Palestinians?*

Using those standards, the answers to any rigorous questioning will actually sharpen, crystallize and elevate the advantages of the Israeli Palestinian Confederation. The following are major objections raised by skeptics:

I
The Confederation does not have legitimacy

The objection is that the Confederation was not created by an official body, such as another government or the United Nations, and therefore has no legitimacy. In reality, most democratic governments are first created and formed by a group of individuals or a private organization and only subsequently recognized by other governments or international organizations. This includes Israel's government and that of the U.S., both of which obtained their legitimacy from the people and from other countries and the international community. When an autocracy becomes a democracy, it is usually done by a revolution spearheaded by a group of individuals who later obtain their legitimacy from the people they wish to govern and from the international community.

Since the Israeli Palestinian Confederation will be the government of the people of Israel and Palestine, it will be they who give it legitimacy by voting in the elections. It will be up to the elected Parliament members, the president and the vice president to seek legitimacy from the international community.

II
The Confederation has no precedent

The geographic location of the Israeli-Palestinian dispute, the nature of the conflict and its historical development are unique. The concept of a confederation, however, is not new. Confederations are designed to help two or more groups of people who live together manage their affairs in a civilized manner despite their hostility and suspicion. This system becomes attractive when the groups finally realize that they are here to stay and they are not able to get rid of each other. It becomes a practical solution when they realize that cooperating with each other is the most productive option they have. Each confederation or federal system is unique; each is dependent on its geography and the makeup of its people. A confederation is not a preset, one-size-fits-all prescription. The principle, however, remains the same. A confederation is a common government working together with the separate governments based on a set of rules with the purpose of reaching mutually acceptable results.

Former Massachusetts governor and U.S. presidential candidate Michael Dukakis, who appeared at one of our symposia, compared the Israeli Palestinian Confederation to the multinational European Union, an intergovernmental union of 25 states, each maintaining its own identity. Since its establishment in 1992, the EU has conducted an election every five years for the European Parliament. The EU manages to maintain a common government for all of the 25 states, yet each one of them has its own separate government.

Switzerland has two chambers in the legislative branch, the National Council representing the people, and the Council of States representing the cantons. The Swiss National Council has 200 seats, with each canton contributing representatives in proportion to its size. The Council of States has two members for each canton and one member for a half-canton. The Swiss system is meant to create a balance in which the small cantons will be protected from the large.

The U.S. and Canada have a formula that combines a federal government overlapping with separate state governments. In the U.S., each of the 50 states has its own constitution and legislative body. However, each state sends two senators and a proportionate number of congressional representatives, depending on its population size, to a common federal government.

The idea of a confederation is widely accepted around the world. It is designed to achieve cooperation while preserving the identity and special needs of its states.

III

The Confederation is a risk to the Jewish state

Some skeptics claim that the Confederation may be dangerous to the Jewish state because it includes Palestinians as well as Israelis and elevates the political power of the Palestinians. Israel's current Arab population, combined with the Arab population in the West Bank and Gaza, exceeds the Jewish population within the same geographic location. The concern for the Jewish state is that the Confederation government may be able to pass legislation that will work against the Jewish state.

The Arab population in Israel, the West Bank and Gaza is likely to grow and outnumber the Israeli or Jewish population regardless of whether the Confederation exists. The Confederation Constitution recognizes the government of Israel as a separate government for the Israeli people and the government of Palestine as the separate government for the Palestinian people.

A reading of the Confederation Constitution will show that the government of Israel and the Israeli Parliament could veto any legislation passed by the Confederation. According to Article I, Section 2, "No bill shall become law unless 55 percent of the Palestinian and 55 percent of the Israeli members of Parliament have passed it, and unless the respective Israeli and Palestinian heads of governments and the separate Israeli and Palestinian legislative bodies have been given a reasonable and equal opportunity to veto said bill, and unless said governments and legislative bodies decline to veto such legislation within a reasonable time as prescribed by the bill."

This part of the Constitution was specifically designed to encourage consensus and to prevent the majority from riding roughshod over the minority. Even assuming that someday the Israelis will be a minority, under the Confederation Constitution they will be protected since the Constitution requires a yes vote by 55 percent of the Israeli members of Parliament and gives the Israeli head of state and the Israeli legislature a veto power over the legislation.

From Israel's point of view, there are two likely scenarios developing in their relationship with the Palestinians.

In the first scenario, the two states are established. Once established, a confederation between these two states will be the mechanism to manage their relationships and help them maintain peace and grow successfully into the future. A confederation will help both sides maintain economic and civic relations. It will aid communication and reduce tension. It will help in the everyday conflicts between the two states. Clearly, the Israeli Palestinian Confederation will be beneficial to both countries if and when they become two states.

The second scenario is that the status quo will continue, and the Palestinians will remain occupied by the Israelis. In this scenario, the Palestinian people do not have their own state and are not part of the state of Israel. The Israeli military continues to be the dominant force restricting the Palestinians. In light of the several Palestinian intifadas and the democratic revolution in the Arab world, this scenario is risky for the Israelis because the Palestinians will see Israel as an autocracy that needs to be toppled exactly as other Arab leaders have been toppled. Should the status quo remain the same for years to come, the Palestinians will be the majority population in the region and are very likely to revolt against Israel. Even under this second scenario, a confederation government provides some constitutional relief to the Palestinians and will likely relieve the pressure on Israel from the Palestinians.

Without a confederation, Israel's current policy towards the Palestinians creates the highest risk to the continued existence of a Jewish state.

IV
The Confederation is not in the long-term interest of the Palestinians

This notion that the Israeli Palestinian Confederation is not in the long-term interests of the Palestinian people was suggested to me by Palestinian-American attorney Stephen Mashney, who claimed that in the long run the Palestinians will outnumber the Israelis and will be able to force a one-state solution on Israel.

First, the Confederation cannot prevent the Palestinian population from growing. If a one-state solution is the ultimate destiny of the region, a confederation is not an obstacle to such a solution. The Confederation deals with the region as it is now. The Confederation is a mechanism to assist the Palestinians achieve equality and improve their lives today. Currently, all aspects of the status of the Palestinian people must be improved. It is utterly irresponsible to suggest to an entire nation that their salvation will not be coming in their lifetimes. Any responsible plan for peace should be aimed at the present with immediate positive effects on its people.

Second, what guarantee does anyone have about the future in 50 to 100 years? Do we know with certainty what the nature of the region will be at that time? The Palestinians' interest is to make peace with Israel today and not to wait 50 years. Should the Palestinian people make peace with Israel, their daily life will improve substantially. They will have freedom of movement and religion, better economic and civic opportunities. They will be able to practice their religion freely at any religious site they wish without interference. They will not be humiliated by the occupation and will be able to enjoy all the benefits afforded free citizens all over the world. To suggest that their long-term interest is to remain isolated and at odds with Israel for a speculative benefit beyond their lifetimes is contrary to common sense.

V

The Confederation is a good idea after the creation of the two-state solution, not before

This is the most common objection voiced by skeptics. The argument usually goes like this: "You don't put the cart before the horse." The implication is that the Confederation makes sense only after the creation of the two states, not before.

The better metaphor is that a person who is about to undergo a major surgery should eat well and exercise before the operation. No responsible surgeon will ever tell the patient that he can eat junk food and remain a couch potato prior to surgery, that he should only start paying attention to his health after the surgery. Currently, we do not have a two-state solution. The Confederation is needed before and after the two states are created.

The Israelis and the Palestinians have been trying to come up with a two-state solution since 1948. The United Nations voted for the establishment of the two states in 1947. It is about time for an alternative resolution that is not in conflict with those attempts.

The Confederation does not stand in the way of the creation of the two states. In fact, the Confederation Parliament, comprised of Israelis and Palestinians "seated together" on a daily basis and working over the Internet to develop legislation, may agree that a two-state solution is the best solution. However, the Parliament could also come up with so many immediate (and interim) steps toward peace that it is utterly irresponsible to suggest that all other efforts should remain on hold until the two states are created.

The Confederation Parliament will be comprised of individuals representing their district, not the entire nation of Israel or Palestine. Within a short time after they are sworn into office, the members will start meeting on a regular basis, developing rapport and eventually trust. They will come up with innovative and new methods to make peace. To suggest that they should hold off until the two states are created simply does not make sense and is just as preposterous as the suggestion that they should wait until the one state is established.

VI
Israelis and Palestinians are culturally different

This argument relies on the myth that Israelis and Palestinians are so different culturally that they are not able to share the same government.

Most Israeli Jews are immigrants or descendants of Jews from Arab states. They share the same culture and speak the same languages as the Muslim and Christian Palestinians. About 20 percent of Israelis are Muslims who also share the same culture and religion as the Palestinians in the West Bank and Gaza.

Most Jews from Arab and European countries came from non-democratic backgrounds, and most did not cast a single vote until they immigrated to Palestine or Israel. The Palestinians also came from a non-democratic background and did not cast a single vote for their government until after the creation of the state of Israel. Most Jews from Arab and European countries, as well as Israeli Arabs and Palestinian Arabs in the West Bank and Gaza, are secular. A substantial number of Palestinian and Israeli Arabs speak Hebrew, and a substantial number of Israelis speak Arabic.

Within their own communities, even the religious Jews and Muslims share common values and the same anti-secular feelings.

The cultures of the people of Israel and Palestine are quite similar. They share the same habits, music, food, language and beliefs. Differences in culture never prevented Israelis of Arab descent from getting along with Israelis of European descent. Culture never stood as an obstacle to Israeli Arabs getting along with Israeli Jews. Muslims and Jews lived in peace for hundreds of years in Arab countries. The dividing line between Israelis and Palestinians is national and not cultural. The conflict stems from the differences between Palestinians and Israelis on the creation of the state of Israel and on maintaining it as a Jewish state.

The Israeli Palestinian Confederation will create a mutual nationalism for the Israelis and the Palestinians to share while at the same time providing each the opportunity to maintain their own separate identity and separate nationalism.

VII

The governments of Israel and Palestine could pass the same legislation, so there is no need for the Confederation

This argument holds that there is no need to create a confederation because the independent governments of Israel or Palestine could either pass the same laws by themselves or enter into a treaty with each other to achieve results similar to laws that would be passed by the proposed Confederation.

The operative word is "could," and it is critical. The reality is that they have not done so for more than 60 years. These governments are in opposition to each other. As adversaries, they have kept the level of cooperation to a minimum. When each government passes legislation on its own, it rarely considers the other side. Their dealings with each other have been limited to the division of real estate and to assigning blame when security is breached. These two governments have not risen to any significant level of generosity, open-heartedness or philanthropy toward one another. They are supported by nationalistic constituencies that demand victory over the other side. They have never developed a culture of cooperation with each other. They treat each other with pettiness and suspicion. They think defensively and cautiously. Even when they negotiate with each other, their main concern is how to outmaneuver or outsmart the other. If one side makes a proposal, the other side immediately becomes defensive and views the move as a ploy. This kind of relationship is not conducive to achieve greatness. It is a relationship that fosters rigidity and obstinacy.

The Israeli and Palestinian governments are usually weak. They spend most of their time fighting for survival. They spend much time handling their economic and security concerns and do not spend much time with each other. Their ability to come up with any legislation or treaty that will benefit the other side is limited.

The Confederation changes the constellation of the relationship between the Palestinian and the Israeli peoples. Instead of being in opposition to each other, they are now on the same side. Instead of being the chess players trying to outfox each other, they are now the orchestra players seated next to each other with the shared goal of making music together.

An Israeli or Palestinian member of the Confederation Parliament will have primary responsibility to his or her district. The member's primary concern is, "What effect will my vote have on my district?" She does not necessarily consider her vote in terms of her nationality because she knows that under the Confederation Constitution her national government is responsible for the national interest of her people. The interests of her district may very well align with the interests of another Parliament member's district. Israeli and Palestinian members of Parliament may thus vote the same way despite the difference in their citizenship.

In addition to the change of approach from adversarial to cooperative, the Confederation provides its Parliament members more flexibility and a greater ability to resolve issues, advantages that are not available to the separate Israeli or Palestinian governments. Since by definition the Israeli Palestinian Confederation is made up of Israelis and Palestinians, it can attempt to deal with issues in a completely different way than would the separate governments of Israel or Palestine.

Right now, the government of Israel deals with the governments of Iran, Hamas, Hezbollah, Syria and other countries as adversaries. Israel is limited in its dealings with those countries. It can only exchange threats with them and attempt to effect change in their behavior by intimidating them. Again, this is a very limited and rigid method that can easily escalate into war. Countries and heads of state do not like to change their behavior as a result of intimidation. Israel has only one arrow in its quiver when it comes to dealing with those governments.

The Confederation has completely different tools. It will have no military and cannot intimidate those countries. However, the Confederation has the power of the people of Israel and Palestine together, a tool not available to the separate Israeli or Palestinian governments.

The Confederation Parliament members will also have the luxury of picking and choosing the legislation they want to tackle. They do not necessarily have to tackle the most difficult issue first. Since they do not have a nationalistic or national agenda, they could pass the most mundane legislation on what may be viewed as insignificant issues. Gradually they can develop trust among themselves and find methods and systems to solve more controversial issues.

In contrast, the separate Israeli and Palestinian governments must first deal with the most controversial issues, mainly the division of land. This issue is so enormous and the tools available for these governments are so archaic that they fail every time they try. Needless to say, when the separate Israeli and Palestinian governments fail to reach an agreement on the bigger issues, they tend to pull apart while blaming each other for the failure, making the process even less conducive to reaching resolution on the mundane issues.

In short, the Confederation has a better system, better ground rules and a better mechanism for reaching agreement. It has been designed for that purpose and has the flexibility and agility to formulate legislation in a manner not now available to the separate Israeli or Palestinian governments.

VIII
The governments of Israel and Palestine will ignore the Confederation

This argument is that the governments of Israel and Palestine have not sanctioned the Israeli Palestinian Confederation and therefore have no obligation to accept or reject any of its legislation. The merits of this argument will depend on the level of support the Confederation government can garner. The more domestic and internal support the Confederation has, the less these governments will be able to ignore the Confederation.

Should there be significant support for the Confederation's upcoming elections, the governments of Israel and Palestine will have an extremely hard time justifying to their people, and indeed to the entire world, their unwillingness to accept the Confederation as a viable path to peace.

The Confederation government provides a reasonable solution for both sides. Once a government chooses to ignore its own people and a reasonable solution for peace, it loses its legitimacy. It will not be able to claim that it left no stone unturned. A government that ignores its own people and a reasonable prospect for peace will have difficulty recruiting its young to fight for her. It will have a hard time persuading other governments that its aim is for peace. It may lose international support and could become a pariah state.

Both the governments of Israel and Palestine are extremely sensitive to their international and domestic images. Currently, they are still able to blame each other for the failure to make peace. However, once the Israeli Palestinian Confederation government becomes a reality, those governments will enter a completely different playing field. They will discover that their own citizens are developing alternative means to reach peace in a way that is fair for both sides. At that point, they will not be able to shift the blame to their own citizens who are participating in the Confederation. They will therefore decide that the more advantageous option is to cooperate with the Confederation government rather than to ignore it.

Recognition of the Confederation by the Israeli and the Palestinian governments is not necessarily the ultimate blessing. It may even be that a pure Israeli Palestinian Confederation without input from the separate governments will be more conducive for peace. The Confederation government might develop a system of cooperative implementation without the need to engage the separate governments. Just as a patient can learn to eat well, exercise and improve his health without the blessing of his surgeon, so the Confederation might learn to adopt and pass legislation without the need to involve those governments.

Recognition of the Confederation by the Israeli and the Palestinian governments is not by any means the ultimate success of the Confederation. The Confederation should establish itself with the people who support it now. It should learn to function with or without the recognition of the separate governments of Israel and Palestine. It should lead the way for smart and progressive legislation that in time will capture the hearts and minds of the people and their governments.

IX
Republicans and Democrats do not get along, so how could the Israelis and the Palestinians?

The implication of this argument is that if people of the same country but different parties cannot reach agreement, how could people of different countries, let alone enemies, sit in the same government?

In reality, Republicans and Democrats do get along. Any visit to a federal law library will confirm that they have been able to pass thousands of statutes. The vast federal system functions on a daily basis because over time Republicans and Democrats have reached consensus. They always seem not to get along—until they do. One reason is that at the end of the day each member of Congress represents his or her district or state. They do not represent the whole country or even their party. They represent only their district or state. At the end of each term, he or she must show results. It is hard to show results unless you are willing to cooperate.

The thousands of statutes, rules and regulations passed by Congress are all a product of compromise. The federal statutes passed by Congress are not the product of love between legislators. They are the product of a system prescribed by the U.S. Constitution, which requires, and indeed forces, the legislators to play ball and compromise.

Using this principle of cooperation, the Confederation Constitution requires its legislators to participate in the process and to compromise. It requires 55 percent of the Israeli and 55 percent of the Palestinian members of Parliament to vote in favor of any legislation before it can be submitted to the separate Israeli and Palestinian heads of state and legislatures. Under the Confederation Constitution, neither the Israeli nor the Palestinian members of Parliament can pass legislation without cooperation from each other.

The current mistrust between Israelis and Palestinians is a product of an adversarial relationship based on nationalism. It is natural that enemies will not trust each other. The Confederation, however, turns the tables. It creates a system in which they are not enemies but rather must cooperate with each other.

X
The Confederation interferes with the sovereignty of Israel and Palestine

The argument is that the Israeli Palestinian Confederation amounts to an imposition of laws and jurisdictions on the Israeli and Palestinian governments and therefore interferes with those governments' sovereignty.

Their sovereignty is not at risk because the preamble to the Constitution specifically states, "The Israeli Palestinian Confederation does not intend to supersede or supplant the Palestinian or Israeli governments, nor to abrogate or undermine any agreements between those governments."

The Constitution's Article I, Section 2 states, "No bill shall become law unless 55 percent of the Palestinian and 55 percent of the Israeli members of Parliament have passed it, and unless the respective Israeli and Palestinian heads of governments and the separate Israeli and Palestinian legislative bodies have been given a reasonable and equal opportunity to veto said bill, and unless said governments and legislative bodies decline to veto such legislation within a reasonable time as prescribed by the bill."

Section 20 of Article I states, "The laws of the Palestinian government and the laws of the Israeli government shall be the supreme law of the land; any conflict of laws between the Israeli or Palestinian governments and the Confederation shall be interpreted to allocate superior weight to the separate Israeli or Palestinian governments."

It is clear from the Constitution that the Confederation could not and does not intend to pass laws that are in conflict with the laws of the state of Israel or Palestine. Those separate governments have a veto power over any legislation passed by the Confederation that affects their states. In addition, laws passed by the Confederation could not override any laws passed by the separate governments. With all these measures of protection, it is unlikely that Confederation laws will infringe on the sovereignty of those governments.

Despite those protections, the separate governments may consent to limited infringements on their sovereignty as is done regularly by most modern countries around the world. Governments permit infringement on their sovereignty when they allow international organizations, such as the United Nations, to house their offices in their territories, or allow foreign embassies to be built in their country, or allow foreign airlines to fly over their air space. Consensual infringements of sovereignty are necessary for countries to advance their own interests in dealing with other foreign interests. It is fully expected that the governments of Israel and Palestine will adhere to the same standards.

XI
Palestinians and Israelis who reside outside the area cannot participate in the elections

Some Palestinians have objected to the residency requirement in the Constitution that allows voting only by those citizens who reside in Palestine. Their concern is that the Palestinian refugees who live outside Israel or Palestine are unable to participate in the Confederation's elections. This residency restriction also applies to Israeli citizens who do not reside in Israel.

Neither the Israeli nor the Palestinian government allows access to the ballot box to citizens who are not residents. The Confederation's similar restriction does not diverge from the norm. In addition, the residency requirement makes even more sense for the Confederation than it does for the separate governments because the Confederation's elections are based on districts. Voters vote and candidates run based on their district of residence. It would not make sense for a person who is not a resident of a district to vote or run in that district.

XII
The Confederation was originated by a group outside the area

This objection is that an outside group is the sponsor of the elections. The implication is that an outside group is not qualified to dictate a solution for the Israeli or the Palestinian people.

The Israeli-Palestinian conflict is no longer a local issue. Many Jews, Muslims and Christians worldwide have substantial connections to the area and to the conflict. Israeli and Palestinian leaders often recruit the help of supporters from outside the area to advance their cause. The conflict has spread so far that people who have no ties to the region get involved in it. The conflict has substantial effect on world peace and the global economy. Innocent people get sucked into the conflict and pay for it with their lives. This conflict ceased to be local more than a century ago. A resolution of this conflict will have a ripple effect on the entire region and the world.

The reality is that for several decades many outsiders have regularly influenced the region. They include major organizations, governments and individuals. Indeed, the very idea of establishing a Jewish state was conceived by an outside person and outside groups. In most cases, opposition to an outside group comes from only those people who oppose the policy of the outside group. Rarely do people oppose an outside group that supports their cause.

The idea of a confederation should be judged only on its merits and not on who conceived of it, just as a treatment for cancer or other ailment is judged on its merits and not on the citizenship of the people who discovered it or where they resided when the discovery was made. The important thing is that the idea would be implemented exclusively by Israelis and Palestinians who reside in the area. Only Israelis and Palestinians who meet the criteria set forth in the Constitution can vote and participate in this new government. This will help the local Israeli and Palestinian people shape their destiny.

XIII
Internet elections are not reliable

The objection is that Internet voting conducted on a website is not reliable and cannot be the basis upon which a government is elected. A deeper look into this issue will reveal that the likelihood of fraud in these elections is slim, and that the Internet is the only way the voting could take place.

First, it should be noted that the upcoming elections to create the Israeli Palestinian Confederation are not only unique because they will happen exclusively on the Internet, they are the first elections in which Israelis and Palestinians will participate together. It is the first time in history that both Israelis and Palestinians have found a common formula for peace. It is the first time that Israelis and Palestininians are rising up as a people, independent of their governments, and taking action for peace. It is the first time in history that both are accepting the same Constitution and both are swearing an allegiance to the same Constitution. It is the first time in history that both Israelis and Palestinians are willing to serve in the same government as equals.

These remarkable strides could only have come because of the Internet. The Internet helped connect those Israelis and Palestinians who agreed on the same formula for peace.

Second, because these are the first Confederation elections and the candidates are volunteers who will not even be paid for their public service, the likelihood of anyone wanting to interfere is minimal. No one has the motivation to commit fraud in order to facilitate the election of person Y over person X. What is important is that the elections take place and that there are candidates and voters who are willing to sit together once elected.

Third, we have taken measures to prevent both duplicative registration and registration by people outside the region. The more likely scenario is that we may not fully detect candidates or voters who do not meet Constitutional requirements, such as age and district residence. However, this will be apparent immediately after the elections and subject to correction in accordance with the Constitution.

Fourth, we have allowed a long period of time, more than two years, for candidates and voters to register. This will assure that as many people who want to participate can, even if they do not own a computer. All they have to do is go to a library or a friend's house or an Internet café to register as a voter or candidate.

Fifth, in the same spirit, the voting itself will start on December 12, 2012, and will end on December 31, 2012. This period of almost three weeks will allow anyone who wants to vote to do so.

XIIII

Recent developments put the idea of the Confederation into question

Three major developments that may have an impact on the conflict have occurred or are forthcoming at the time this book was being written. The first is the apparent reconciliation between Hamas and Fatah. The second is the anticipated United Nations vote to recognize a Palestinian state within recognized borders. The third is an anticipated Palestinian election in 2012. These events will only crystallize and reaffirm the need for the Confederation.

For more than 60 years, while the Israelis and Palestinians went through tremendous internal shifts in politics, the need to resolve the conflict between the two governments remained constant. The Confederation will be an independent entity. It will be a mechanism to solve issues between these two governments, regardless of whether the Palestinians or the Israelis are themselves internally divided or united.

Should the U.N. vote again to recognize a Palestinian state within a recognizable border and should that state actually be established, both sides would need a framework to manage the relationship between the two states. The Confederation could be that framework, one that will deal with the relationship based on legislation. The Parliament will meet daily on the Internet for the purpose of managing the relationship. It will require the consent of 55 percent of the Israeli and 55 percent of the Palestinian members of Parliament to agree on a resolution. Once they agree, the separate Israeli and the Palestinian legislative bodies and heads of state will have a veto power over the legislation.

Given the historical hostility between the Israelis and Palestinians, they will not be able to manage their relationship fairly without a confederation. Even if the U.S. or the U.N. sends troops to keep the peace between the two states, those troops will only be able to make sure that the two sides refrain from hostility. The U.S. or the U.N. will not be able stay in the region forever. Both sides will trip and trick the peacekeepers regularly to gain an advantage.

Peace is a product of hard work and nourishment by the people themselves. They must grow and learn to deal with each other as equals. They must work hard every day and deal with all the issues separating them. They must have a fair and balanced mechanism with acceptable rules to resolve those issues. The Confederation will provide them with those tools. One of our board members, Ferial Masry, correctly pointed out that the revolutions in the Arab world made people nervous because of the unknown outcome of those revolutions. There were no alternative democratic bodies that the system could rely on once the revolutions began. The Israeli Palestinian Confederation will provide a democratic system as a safety net to protect the relationship between the Israelis and the Palestinians.

CHAPTER EIGHT

12-12-12

On December 12, 2012, for the first time in history, Israelis and Palestinians will be able to vote for a confederation government that will represent both peoples. Three hundred Parliament members from Palestine and Israel will be elected. These elected members will sit together as equals and draft legislation for peace. Israeli and Palestinian voters will also elect the Confederation president and vice president, who will rotate their offices after two years so that a Palestinian will be president for half a term, an Israeli for the other half.

This momentous event could change history, but both Palestinians and Israelis need international support to help make the Confederation government a reality. This is particularly true when it comes to those courageous individuals who are willing to put their safety and personal reputations on the line by running as the first officers of the Israeli Palestinian Confederation.

You have a unique opportunity to help make this a reality. Please visit our website at www.ipconfederation.org and contact the candidates. Encourage them to continue their effort. Tell them they are doing the right thing for peace and how much you appreciate their work. Contact the media in your community and tell them about the Israeli Palestinian Confederation and its alternative way to make peace. Ask your congressional representative and your senators to endorse the idea of a confederation. Ask your candidate for the presidency of the U.S. to state his or her opinion on the Israeli Palestinian Confederation. Do not just let them get away with an answer that a confederation is a good idea after the Israelis and the Palestinians reach the two-state solution. Ask them why is it not a good idea now. Take it upon yourself to educate people about this solution. Do not let the skeptics discourage you. Ask them for their plan for peace. Tell them that the Confederation is not against any other plan for peace, but only an additional method for achieving that goal. The truth is that the only people who can resolve the issue are the people of Israel and Palestine. They are the ones who live together and know the area. They are the ones who will continue to live together forever. No foreign government or army will be able to impose peace on them. Peace is an intricate venture that requires good faith and vision from both sides. It requires people to sit together as equals to come up with an acceptable formula. It requires a mechanism to achieve the formula. The Israeli Palestinian Confederation has that mechanism. But it is not enough. A good idea is meaningless unless it is properly implemented. Once the Confederation receives legitimacy from people in the community and from people it respects, support will follow.

All we need do is to encourage 1 percent or 2 percent of eligible Israeli and Palestinian voters to say yes to the idea. This would mean that more than 100,000 people, both Israelis and Palestinians, are willing to work together based on an acceptable formula. This will force the issue. Never before in history have Israelis and Palestinians agreed on a similar formula. No longer will their governments be able to blame each other and get away with it. No longer will they be able to claim that their solution is the only solution. No longer will they be able to justify war because "there are no other solutions." Their leaders will have to explain why they are rejecting the Confederation. Their leaders will have to explain to the parents of the victims the reasons for their child's death. They will have to explain to the soldier who lost a leg why they failed to make peace. Why was it necessary to continue with the same tired military solution when there was a reasonable resolution by way of a confederation? How will those leaders answer the parents of those victims?

> "Mr. Leader, before you sent my son to die, did you think about the idea of a confederation?"
> "Yes, I thought it was a naïve idea. I thought it would not work, and therefore I objected to this idea."
> "Have you tried this idea of a confederation to make peace?"
> "No."

"What is the basis upon which you decided that it is not going to work?"
"I had no basis. All I know is that I cannot trust the enemy, and they would have never cooperated."
"Mr. Leader, you said that you want peace and that you would not leave any stone unturned for peace."
"Correct. I want peace but the other side does not, and it takes two to tango."
"So, what exactly did you mean when you said that you will not leave any stone unturned for peace? You failed to turn this stone. You failed to do so because you have a limited vision for peace. I lost my son believing that there was no choice, but it turned out that there was a choice, and you simply refused to believe in it."

In order to force the governments to fear not making the choice, we have to make the choice a reality. The governments of Israel and Palestine will not even acknowledge the existence of this choice unless we have a groundswell of support. The one thing all governments are afraid of is public opinion.

Both the Israeli and Palestinian governments want to appear reasonable. Right now they get away with appearing reasonable by blaming each other. They will not, however, be able to appear reasonable when they reject a plan that calls for a balanced approach that gives them veto power. They will not be able to appear reasonable when the media and respected leaders endorse a confederation. They will not be able to appear reasonable by criticizing their own citizens who are participating in the Confederation as Parliament members or who voted for the Confederation. They will not be able to appear reasonable when they reject legislation that benefits their own citizens and advances the cause of peace.

Once the idea of the Confederation gains momentum, it will have a snowball effect. We need you now to create the momentum. Please take the time to support us. We also need financial support. We have a huge task ahead of us in educating the public and the media about the intricacies of this program. We need to show the citizens of Israel and Palestine that this program does not contradict their national aspiration or basic values, that they can maintain the love for their country, and that their country will remain the same, only stronger and in peace. We need to respond to the vast amount of disinformation that is being spread about this plan. Many Israelis and Palestinians genuinely want peace. They could end up supporting this program if they have the right information and are able to debate it. This is your opportunity to be part of history and not just observe it happening. Do what you can to help.

The Constitution of the Israeli Palestinian Confederation

Preamble

The peoples of Palestine and Israel, in order to bring about peace and prosperity, establish justice, ensure domestic tranquility, promote the general welfare, and secure liberty for ourselves and our posterity, do ordain and establish this Constitution for the Israeli Palestinian Confederation.

The Israeli Palestinian Confederation serves as a government of the people to resolve conflicts and grow into the future in a fair and equitable manner.

We believe that Palestinians and Israelis are entitled to live at peace and enjoy liberty, the pursuit of happiness, and self-determination.

We believe that Palestinians and Israelis are entitled to equal rights under the law, and guaranteed human rights and freedom.

We believe that the creation of a confederation is consistent with the aspirations of the peoples of Palestine and Israel. The Israeli Palestinian Confederation does not intend to supersede or supplant the Palestinian or Israeli governments, nor to abrogate or undermine any agreements between those governments.

We believe that the principles stated above will be achieved through the facilities of a mutual confederation, dedicated to fair representation of both the Israeli and the Palestinian peoples, and dedicated to achieving consensus through confederation principles.

ARTICLE I

Section 1. All legislative powers herein granted shall be vested in the Parliament, which shall consist of a combined 300 Palestinian and Israeli members elected within Israel and Palestine. Said Parliament shall be called the Israeli Palestinian Parliament. The time, place, and manner of the Parliament's legislative sessions and voting mechanism shall be prescribed by the Parliament.

The time, place, and manner of holding elections, subsequent to the first, shall be prescribed by the Parliament. For the purpose of conducting the first elections, districts shall be drawn by the founding committee prior to the elections.

The founding committee shall prescribe the time, place, and manner of the first elections for the President, Vice President, and members of Parliament, as well as the time, place, and manner for the first Parliament to conduct its legislative sessions.

Subsequent to the first elections, the 300 districts shall be set by an independent committee composed of Israelis and Palestinians who meet the eligibility requirement to vote in the upcoming elections, and who shall not run as candidates in those elections. The committee shall be appointed in accordance with the Appointment Clause of Article I, Section 24.

Districts shall be drawn randomly based on population. Districts may be drawn in blocks that include several districts, or may be drawn to accommodate the various natural and man-made geographic features.

The committee shall announce the districts at least 180 days prior to the elections. Districts may change at each election to reflect a change in population or in geographical features. The committee shall attempt to assign districts to reflect the entire population. Said committee shall be allowed sufficient latitude in drawing the districts to promote whatever practical and efficient innovation will best accommodate free and fair elections.

Section 2. No bill shall become law unless 55 percent of the Palestinian and 55 percent of the Israeli members of Parliament have passed it, and unless the respective Israeli and Palestinian heads of governments and the separate Israeli and Palestinian legislative bodies have been given a reasonable and equal opportunity to veto said bill, and unless said governments and legislative bodies decline to veto such legislation within a reasonable time as prescribed by the bill. No bill shall prescribe a period of fewer than 30 days unless said bill is declared an emergency bill, and unless a fair, equal, and reasonable opportunity is afforded to the Israeli and Palestinian heads of government and legislative bodies to veto said legislation.

Prior to the enforcement of any law, the Confederation shall obtain an approved petition from the Israeli or Palestinian governments authorizing it to enforce said law within the jurisdiction of the authorizing government.

Section 3. The Parliament may pass laws designating the time, place, and manner of issuance of vetoes, as well as the identities of those governments and legislative bodies on whom a veto power is bestowed.

Section 4. Laws not affecting the separate Israeli or Palestinian governments may pass upon a 55 percent vote of the Palestinian and 55 percent of the Israeli members of Parliament and shall not be subject to veto by those governments.

Section 5. The Parliament shall be composed of members elected every four years by the people of the several districts. Said elections shall take place within the confines of Israel and Palestine. Those eligible to vote must hold citizenship in the state of Israel or in Palestine, as defined by those governments, and must have attained the age of 18, and must reside in Israel or Palestine.

Section 6. A person may be elected to Parliament provided he or she has attained the age of 21 years at the time of the election, and is a citizen of Palestine or Israel, and resides in the district in which he or she may be elected. All Parliament members shall announce their affiliated citizenship upon the announcement of their candidacy, and, when elected, shall be counted as members of the same delegation as their announced citizenship and will remain so until the date of the termination of their term.

A person may announce his or her candidacy for Parliament and President; however, should that person be elected to both, he or she shall make a choice, within 30 days from the date he or she was elected, as to his or her preferred choice of posts. No person shall serve simultaneously as an elected member of the Parliament and in the executive branch of the Confederation.

Section 7. Except for the first elections, the elections for the President, Vice President, and Parliament shall take place at least 30 days prior to the expiration of the term of the current officeholders. Each district shall elect the candidate for Parliament who received the most votes. In the event of a block district that sends several representatives to Parliament, those candidates who receive the most votes shall be elected.

Section 8. When a vacancy occurs in the Parliamentary representation of any district or block of districts, the candidate who received the next highest number of votes for that seat shall be installed. If no such candidate exists, the delegation of which the former representative was a member shall appoint the succeeding representative.

Section 9. Each member of the Parliament shall take the following oath prior to taking office: "I do solemnly swear (or affirm) that I will faithfully execute my duties as a Legislator for the Israeli Palestinian Parliament, and will, to the best of my ability, preserve, protect, and defend the Constitution of the Israeli Palestinian Confederation."

Section 10. Parliament members shall be elected for a period of four years, and each Parliament member shall have one vote. Parliament members shall not serve and shall not be elected for more than 12 years or three terms, whichever is greater.

Section 11. The Parliament shall have the sole power to try and impeach the President and the Vice President, as well as any Parliament members, officers, and Judges of the Confederation. When convening for that purpose, Parliament members shall be on oath or affirmation. When any Confederation government member is tried, one Israeli and one Palestinian member of Parliament shall preside. No person shall be impeached unless 55 percent of the Israeli and 55 percent of the Palestinian members of Parliament have voted for the same article of impeachment. No person shall be convicted unless 65 percent of the Israeli and 65 percent of the Palestinian members of Parliament have voted to convict on the same article.

Section 12. Judgment in cases of impeachment shall not extend beyond removal from office and disqualification to hold and enjoy any office of honor, trust, or profit under the Israeli Palestinian Confederation; but the party convicted shall nevertheless be liable and subject to indictment, trial, judgment, and punishment, according to law.

Section 13. The Parliament shall be the judge of the elections, returns, and qualifications of its own members.

Section 14. The Parliament may determine the rules of its proceedings and punish its members for disorderly behavior.

Section 15. The Parliament shall keep a journal of its proceedings, and from time to time publish the same, and the yeas and nays of the members on any question shall be entered in the journal. The proceedings of the Parliament shall be open to the public, and its proceedings published and available to the general public.

Section 16. The Parliament members shall, in all cases except for treason, felony, and breach of the peace, be privileged from arrest by the Confederation during their attendance at the Parliament, and in going to and returning from the same; and for any speech or debate.

Section 17. Parliament members may receive compensation for their services, to be ascertained by law, and paid from the Confederation treasury.

Section 18. No Parliament member nor the President or Vice President shall simultaneously serve as an elected official in the Israeli or Palestinian governments.

Section 19. The first Parliament shall ratify the Constitution of the Israeli Palestinian Confederation in its present or amended form by a vote of 55 percent of the Israeli and 55 percent of the Palestinian members of Parliament. Any subsequent amendments to the Constitution shall require 65 percent of the Israeli and 65 percent of the Palestinian members of Parliament.

Section 20. The laws of the Palestinian government and the laws of the Israeli government shall be the supreme law of the land; any conflict of laws between the Israeli or Palestinian governments and the Confederation shall be interpreted to allocate superior weight to the separate Israeli or Palestinian governments.

Section 21. The elected and appointed officials of the Israeli Palestinian Confederation government shall be bound by oath or affirmation to support this Constitution; but no religious test shall ever be required as a qualification for any office or public trust under the Israeli Palestinian Confederation.

Section 22. The Israeli Palestinian Confederation shall make no law respecting an establishment of religion, or prohibiting the free exercise thereof; or abridging the freedom of speech, or of the press; or the right of the people peaceably to assemble, and to petition the government for redress of grievances.

Section 23. All debts contracted and obligations entered into by the Confederation, before the adoption of this Constitution, shall be valid against the Confederation.

Section 24. No committee or judicial panel shall be appointed unless an equal number of its members are appointed by the Israeli and the Palestinian delegations to the Parliament, and unless the President and Vice President each have appointed an equal number of the committee or panel members. No person who, at the time of appointment, is a member of the separate Israeli or Palestinian governments, legislative bodies, armies, or police forces shall be appointed. No committee member, judicial officer, or executive appointed on behalf of the Confederation shall take office unless he or she takes the same oath taken by those who made the appointment.

Section 25. The Parliament may override any veto issued by the President of the Confederation by 65 percent of the Israeli and 65 percent of the Palestinian members of Parliament. The Israeli Palestinian Confederation shall not override any veto issued by either the Israeli or the Palestinian governments.

Section 26. This Constitution shall be interpreted based on its English language version.

Section 27. The first election date for the Confederation government shall be December 12, 2012, and shall last for a period of time as shall be announced by the Confederation founding committee. Said elections and future elections may be conducted in the most convenient manner, including over the Internet, so as to accommodate the needs of the Israeli and Palestinian people.

Section 28. The Confederation government shall be sworn into office within 45 days after the announcement of the election results. The election results shall be certified by the Confederation committee. All elected officials of the Confederation shall take an oath of office, which may be taken verbally, or in writing, or in any manner sufficient to establish a meaningful communication of said oath or affirmation.

Section 29. Any official of the Confederation who was elected in special elections or appointed to office shall serve until the next general elections, and, if qualified, may run in that or any subsequent elections.

ARTICLE II

Section 1. The executive power of the Confederation shall be vested in a President and Vice President for a term of four years. The President shall hold his or her office during the term of two years, and shall alternate at the expiration of the two years with the Vice President, who shall become the President in the second two years of the term; at that point the previous President shall become Vice President. The President and the Vice President shall be elected at the same time. Said President and Vice President shall be citizens and residents of Israel or Palestine.

The President and Vice President shall be elected every four years during the general elections held at the same time as the elections for Parliament. The candidate who obtains the most votes from the entire pool of voters for President shall be elected as President for the first two years of the term. The Vice President shall be of a different citizenship from the person elected President. The person of a different citizenship from the President who received the second largest number of votes from the entire pool of voters shall be elected as Vice President and shall serve as such for of the first two years of the term.

Section 2. The President shall have the power to veto legislation passed by the Confederation Parliament at any time prior to a veto issued by the separate Israeli or Palestinian governments.

The President may issue executive orders, which will be in effect for a period of 90 days, to facilitate the President's and Vice President's executive duties. Said orders shall conform to duties bestowed upon him or her by this Constitution or by the Parliament, who may override said orders and regulations by 65 percent of the Israeli and 65 of the Palestinian members of Parliament.

The President shall appoint various secretaries and ministers, who shall be confirmed by 55 percent of the Israeli and 55 percent of the Palestinian members of Parliament. Said secretaries shall take the oath of office as prescribed in this Constitution. A secretary or minister for the Confederation may not act in any official capacity for either the Israeli or Palestinian governments.

The Vice President shall act as the Chief and Commander of the Israeli Palestinian Confederation Police Force. The President shall have the power to enter into treaties with other governments, subject to ratification by the Parliament, and subject to a veto power of the separate Israeli and Palestinian governments as prescribed by Article I, Section 2.

The President and Vice President shall have the power to pardon any individual of all violations relating to laws within the jurisdiction of the Israeli Palestinian Confederation. However, the Parliament shall also have the power to overturn such pardon upon a vote of 55 percent of the Palestinian and 55 percent of the Israeli members of Parliament or upon the vote of 65 percent of either delegation.

Section 3. No President or Vice President shall be elected or serve for more than eight years or two terms, whichever is greater.

Section 4. No person except a citizen and resident of Israel or Palestine shall be eligible to the office of President or Vice President; neither shall any person be eligible for that office who has not attained the age of 35 years.

Section 5. In case of the removal of the President from office, or of his or her death, resignation, or inability to discharge the powers and duties of said office, the same shall be bestowed on the next runner-up candidate for the same office who shall maintain the same rotation, in the elections for the same time period, provided said candidate is of the same citizenship as that of the unavailable President. If no such candidate is available, special elections shall be held within 90 days of the President's declared unavailability. The unavailability of the President shall be declared by the Parliament or by the President himself or herself.

Section 6. In case of the removal of the Vice President from office, or upon his or her death, resignation, or inability to discharge the powers and duties of said office, the same shall be bestowed on the next runner-up candidate for the same office who shall maintain the same rotation, in the elections for the same time period, provided said candidate is of the same citizenship as that of the unavailable Vice President. If no such candidate is available, special elections shall be held within 90 days of the Vice President's declared unavailability. The unavailability of the Vice President shall be declared by the Parliament, or by the Vice President himself or herself.

Section 7. In case of the removal of both the President and Vice President from office, or of the death, resignation, or inability of both the President and Vice President to discharge the powers and duties of said office, the same shall be bestowed on the next runner-up candidates for the same offices for the same time period, who shall maintain the same rotation as that of the unavailable President and Vice President. If no such candidates are available, special elections shall be held within 90 days from their declared unavailability. The unavailability of both the President and the Vice President shall be declared by the Parliament, or by both the President and Vice President.

Section 8. The President and Vice President may, at designated times, receive compensation for their services from the Israeli Palestinian Confederation.

Section 9. Before the President and Vice President enter into the execution of their offices, they shall take the following oath or affirmation: "I do solemnly swear (or affirm) that I will faithfully execute the office of President (or Vice President) of the Israeli Palestinian Confederation, and will to the best of my ability, preserve, protect, and defend the Constitution of the Israeli Palestinian Confederation."

Section 10. The President and Vice President shall have the powers as bestowed upon them by this Constitution and the members of the Israeli Palestinian Parliament, subject to the veto power of the separate Israeli and Palestinian governments, as stated in Article I of this Constitution.

Section 11. The President, Vice President, Parliament members, Judges, and all civil officers of the Israeli Palestinian Confederation, shall be removed from office on impeachment for, and conviction of, treason, bribery, or other high crimes.

Article III

Section 1. The judicial power of the Israeli Palestinian Confederation shall be vested in one Supreme Court and in such lower courts as the Parliament may from time to time ordain and establish. There shall be an equal number of Israeli and Palestinian Judges. Each trial shall contain the same number of Israeli and Palestinian Judges.

All Judges for the Israeli Palestinian Confederation shall be appointed equally by the President and Vice President and shall be confirmed by the Parliament.

In the event of unavailability, a Judge shall be appointed by the President or Vice President of the same citizenship as the unavailable Judge and shall be confirmed by the Parliament.

Section 2. The judicial power shall extend to all cases arising under this Constitution and the laws of the Israeli Palestinian Confederation.

Section 3. All cases shall be heard by an equal number of Israeli and Palestinian Judges. Decisions shall be rendered by a simple majority. In the event a simple majority is unattainable, a random drawing to remove one Judge will be held. However, any legal decision against a Palestinian or Israeli citizen or entity must have a majority of Judges of the same citizenship as that of the person or entity against whom a decision is rendered.

Section 4. All legal decisions, except those relating to the internal operation of the Confederation government, shall have an automatic 60-day stay, and may be appealed to the separate Israeli or Palestinian judicial systems, and may be subject to a complete or partial reversal or modification by the respective Palestinian or Israeli courts in accordance with their laws and requirements. The Israeli Palestinian Confederation decisions relating to the internal operation of the Confederation government shall become final upon a decision of the Israeli Palestinian Confederation Supreme Court.

Section 5. The Israeli Palestinian Confederation judicial system shall give full faith and credit to any legal decision made by the separate Palestinian or Israeli judicial systems.

Definition and usage of words found in the Constitution

Palestine: *West Bank and Gaza*

Israel: *The entire state of Israel that is under the control of the Israeli government*

Israeli Citizen: *A person who is recognized under Israeli law as a citizen of Israel.*

Palestinian Citizen: *A person who is recognized under Palestinian law as a citizen of Palestine.*

Different Citizen: *For an Israeli citizen, a "different citizen" is a Palestinian citizen. For a Palestinian citizen, a "different citizen" is an Israeli citizen.*

Gender: *Masculine or feminine references include both masculine and feminine.*

Acknowledgments

I would like to thank the members of the board of directors of the Israeli Palestinian Confederation, who have encouraged me to go on: Nicholas Allis, Sumner Fein, Dan Henrickson, Abed A. Jlelati, Mohamed Awadalla, Robby Gordon, Ami Magal, David Marcus, Ferial Masry, Aida Porteneuve, Kathleen O'Connor Wang, Harvey Youngman, Aymen Zaben, Oyun Puntsagdorj and Murad Salah. I particularly want to thank my good friend Neil Schwartz, who came up with the idea for this book.

Thanks also to the hundreds of Palestinians and Israelis who have signed up to become candidates for the first Israeli Palestinian Confederation government. You have shown tremendous courage and vision in your willingness to create a more just and peaceful place for the people of Israel and Palestine. You have shown that Israelis and Palestinians can work together to come up with a formula to satisfy the needs and fulfill the dreams of both.

More thanks go to the thousands of people around the globe who communicated with me daily and shared their personal stories, fears and aspirations during our mock Conferation experiment on Facebook. I'm also grateful to the dozens of people who helped by reading every chapter and contributing points of view that made for a better book.

Finally, I want to thank my family, those friends who remained my friends and politely agreed to remember the good old days despite their misgivings about this project, and Mary Ellen Strote, who was hired to edit a book and ended up becoming an advisor and confidant.

About the author

Josef Avesar, an Israeli-born attorney who resides in Southern California, is president of the founding committee of the Israeli Palestinian Confederation. He has conducted numerous symposia on the concept of a confederation between Israelis and Palestinians and has hosted political and civic leaders from around the world in discussions of confederation as a means of resolving the Israeli-Palestinian conflict.
PEACE is his first political book.

CPSIA information can be obtained at www.ICGtesting.com
Printed in the USA
LVOW120355241211

261008LV00001B/40/P